Motivating ELLs

27 Activities

TO INSPIRE & ENGAGE STUDENTS

★Lora Beth ESCALANTE PhD

Published by Seidlitz Education
P.O. Box 166827
Irving, TX 75016
www.seidlitzeducation.com

For related titles and support materials visit www.seidlitzeducation.com.

6.18

Acknowledgments

To all my past, present, and future students: thank you for making me a better educator each and every day.

Kristin Nelson-Steinhoff, your leadership inspired me during a crucial time in my journey. Your infectious smile and genuine care for teachers and students made all the difference. I'll always remember my Schenck Elementary years as the time I fell in love with teaching. I only wish I could have worked with you longer.

When referring to John Seidlitz, I often describe him as my mentor. He leads by example in so many ways. When I initially met him in a professional development training in Boerne, I never imagined I would have the good fortune of working for him a few years later. I was just so excited to try all the strategies the next day in class! It has been an incredible journey. I am profoundly grateful he provided a way for me to get these thoughts in book form to be able to share with teachers. There were a few distractions along the way, such as having a baby and building a house, but he kept me on track.

I am indebted to our dynamite team of editors, Anna and Meg, as well as our graphic design guru, Anne-Charlotte. Thank you all for your patience with me throughout this process! It means so much to me that Dr. Wayne Wright, a talented and passionate professor and prolific author of all things ELL, took the time to read my book and write the foreword.

I thank God for guiding me into teaching and allowing me to experience immeasurable joy working with students, teachers, parents, and administrators. Each day of teaching is resplendent with blessings and challenges and decisions upon decisions to make. It's a tremendous responsibility, and one that I take seriously (with a lot of laughter thrown in, too!).

To *mis gran amores* that motivate my every move: Javier, Sol, Luna, y Enzo. I am so undeserving, but so very grateful for my precious family. My dear parents, Robert and Mira Jubela, who somehow knew I would find my way to teaching.

Los amo con todo mi corazón.

Lora Beth

Table of Contents

FOREWORD

The challenge of motivating students to actively engage in classroom learning is as old as schools themselves. This challenge is even greater when educating students through a language they are not yet fully proficient in. Teachers of English language learners (ELLs) face the double challenge of keeping students motivated to learn English as a new language and to learn academic content through English.

These are important challenges to meet, given that ELLs are one of the fastest growing student groups across the United States. This growth brings great cultural and linguistic diversity into our nation's schools. In the state of Texas, for example, there are more than 850,000 ELLs speaking over one hundred different languages, making up over 15% of the total student population.

Theories of motivation in education in general, and in language learning in particular, are abundant. While scholars conduct research and debate the intricacies of theories and the extent to which they can be put in practice, the voices of actual classroom teachers of ELLs are often ignored, with little regard for their rich experiences working daily with students.

Herein lies the great value of this book by Dr. Lora Beth Escalante, a scholar and teacher trainer who has many years of experience as a former bilingual classroom teacher. She draws on the combination of her academic training and her vast teaching experiences with ELLs to provide a book that teachers will find fully accessible and highly practical. Without overburdening readers with theory and research, this book provides a straightforward framework centered on creating classrooms where ELLs feel welcomed and safe to use their developing language skills for academic purposes, and where their prior knowledge is acknowledged, valued, and built upon to further their English language and academic development. Teachers will likely be highly motivated themselves to read and learn from this book given its personal and friendly writing style and its visually appealing layout and images.

The over two dozen activities featured in this book provide specific strategies, techniques, and lessons teachers can use to build their ELL students' language skills and content knowledge. Also included are activities focused on developing meaningful relationships with students—an important key to motivation that is often neglected.

While the focus on school reform efforts though high-stakes testing and accountability that began with No Child Left Behind (NCLB) continues as we enter the era of the Every Student Succeeds Act (ESSA), it is imperative that teachers resist the types of test-prep focused instruction that has proven effective in demotivating students, and that is particularly harmful for ELLs. I sincerely hope teachers will put into practice the types of instruction and activities highlighted in this book, which hold great potential to create the kinds of classroom environments and instruction that students will find to be highly motivating.

Wayne E. Wright, PhD
Purdue University

My Story *

I wasn't really exposed to different languages or cultures until I went to college. I grew up in Boerne, a small town in central Texas that was comprised of predominantly native English speakers and a small population of English language learners (ELLs). There, I lived on a small farm, and I was used to having farm animals around: cows, chickens, and even some geese! The story of Charlotte's Web was completely relatable to me, as a young girl living on a farm, and I found it exciting because of the talking animals. As a young child, I always thought it would be great to be able to talk to the animals. Actually, I did talk to the animals. It didn't bother me one bit that they didn't talk back. I even took a pet goose to school one day for show and tell.

By the time I decided to try teaching as a profession, I had succeeded at becoming bilingual, though not without a struggle. I began my journey toward bilingualism in high school, motivated by several short-term mission trips to Mexico with my parents and a sensational Spanish teacher. My abilities in my second language soared throughout college as I made friends and socialized with students from Central America. I started carrying on whole conversations with my Nicaraguan roommate in Spanish. Falling in love with a Venezuelan (who is now my husband) didn't hurt either (*tú sabes*, the language of *amor*). I began to check off self-invented milestones: I dreamt in Spanish sometimes, people thought I was a native speaker, I memorized Spanish hymns at church, etc. I will always be a Spanish language learner; it will always be my second language, no matter how rich a vocabulary I acquire or how closely I can imitate a native speaker's accent.

Because of my proficiency, I was given the opportunity to teach in a bilingual classroom in Denver, Colorado while working toward my teacher certification. My bachelor's degree was in marketing, and my only insight into teaching as a profession was watching my father work tirelessly as a math teacher, coach, and bus driver. We would occasionally sit at the dining table and grade papers. My dear father would later remind me how I adamantly declared that I would never become a teacher. It simply involved too many hours and too little pay. Be careful what you say.

When I began teaching, I knew practically nothing about how to teach and even less about how to address the needs of students from different linguistic and cultural groups. I remember sitting down with my very first classroom of third grade students. All these beautiful Hispanic children (who were all English language learners) were looking at me for guidance, and all I could think was, "I can't believe they are leaving me alone with these kids when I don't have a clue what to do." My first classroom, located in the middle of the elementary school building, lacked windows and air conditioning. This would have been more

manageable in Denver had this school not been on a year-round calendar. Mid-July in Denver is very hot. I brought ice cubes from the teachers' lounge and had students rub them on their faces as I read to them. As we rubbed our faces and let the water run down our cheeks, we shared some hearty laughter. I found myself falling in love with those sweet kids. I have since heard several principals say that if you give students good teachers who care for them and are willing to try new things, the students will help those good teachers become great teachers. I've discovered that the teacher-student relationship is of vital importance, as we will discuss in Section 3 of this book, called "Cultivating Relationships." I felt very blessed to be entrusted with these precious children day after day, and I wanted to do right by them and their parents.

Having fond memories of my own from third grade literature, I decided to read them a text that was familiar to me: *Charlotte's Web*. I remember thinking, "I love this book so much, I cannot wait to read this book with my students." So there I was reading *Charlotte's Web* in inner city Denver to a group of immigrant students. The reaction was less than desirable. I had completely failed to consider their background experiences; they were urban students, and most of them actually grew up in Denver. I was just teaching the way I had been taught, modeling my own teaching based on what had been interesting to me as a student. With my small town, rural background, the idea of farm life as it was discussed in Charlotte's Web and the way in which the main character was living was very applicable to my life.

However, this did not apply as well to my English language learners' experiences.

As teachers we should never assume that our students do or do not know, or do or do not have prior knowledge about a certain subject.

The students were not very engaged in the reading, though they were not completely disengaged, as I tried out the instructional strategies I was acquiring in my weekly alternative certification class. We played friendship games with string to represent the words in *Charlotte's Web*. We acted like certain animals from the book. We wrote reflections about certain scenes and chapters. The thought of capturing their attention and holding it was always lingering in my mind. After finishing the novel with the class, I pondered how I could have made *Charlotte's Web* more accessible to my students. I chose this text, but I still struggled. And so often, as teachers, we do not have a choice in selecting what students read. Can we still help students relate to what they're reading and boost engagement? Based on my experience, I believe we can! I explore what has been effective for me and teachers I've worked with in Section 2 of this book, "Bridging Content Connections."

Only later did I realize why my students were not motivated. I completely failed to tap into or access my students' prior knowledge. Even though many of my students had spent their whole lives in the city, several of them did have experiences that helped them relate to *Charlotte's Web*. I found out that some of my students traveled regularly to Mexico to visit their *abuelos* and other relatives on their *ranchos.* These students knew about farm animals, and they did have background knowledge about rural living. I had just asked a bit late. It would have been more

beneficial to have asked before I read the book. Instead I found out after that some of them did have relatable experiences. All of this came up when we were talking about rural versus urban communities in social studies, and those students were able to bring in pictures of scenes from farm life in Mexico. I learned a very valuable lesson that year: as teachers we should never assume that our students do or do not know, or do or do not have prior knowledge about a certain subject.

Later that first year, colleagues introduced me to the idea of using culturally responsive literature. I got my hands on a copy of Sandra Cisneros's *The House on Mango Street* and *Latino Read Aloud Stories.* It completely changed the dynamic of our reading time together. The students could relate to the characters in the stories because they themselves were from similar backgrounds. Even though I might not have been as captivated, I knew it was worth it because my students were so engaged; they were motivated. I learned it was okay to set aside my own interests and explore what captured the kids' minds and hearts. In turn, I broadened my own classroom literary library.

I was given the opportunity the following year to participate in another Denver school's bilingual program. It was there that I was introduced to Francisco Jimenez's *The Circuit.* His short stories reflected experiences that my Hispanic immigrant students could relate to. They read about kids from their own age group and similar cultural background. Meanwhile, I was blessed with an opportunity to work toward a master's degree in multicultural education and ESL through a teacher cohort with the University of Colorado in Boulder. We met weekly in different Denver public schools, and we acquired very practical strategies to use each week with our own students. It was through these gifted professors (Diana Geisler, Kathy Escamilla, and Janeatte Klingner, to name a few) that I was motivated to pursue a doctoral degree. I hoped someday I would be able to encourage and inspire teachers the way these university professors were inspiring me.

Several years later I began my doctoral degree in San Antonio, Texas, while also working as a teacher in an elementary school in my hometown of Boerne. As a fourth grade dual-language teacher, I noticed my English language learners, in particular, found the history lessons abstract and unrelatable. How could I motivate my students to dive into Texas history and enjoy the ride? Fortunately, about the same time I was struggling with my new role, I had the opportunity to attend trainings on the SIOP® model (Echeverria, Vogt, & Short, 2016). It was through these half-day workshops, spread over several months, that I developed the idea of working through history with one-act plays. I designed the group interactional aspect, that formed the basis for my dissertation research, around the concepts and activities I learned during these trainings. Students could take on the roles of famous Texas history figures and really understand what it was like to live in different time periods.

Through the simulation and the creative process of developing one-act plays

with their peers, my ELL fourth graders' engagement level seemed to shoot up overnight. As students in my classroom were working through ideas and developing their scripts, they were constantly flowing between listening to each other, speaking about their ideas and suggestions, writing down portions of the script, and reading as they referred back to resources such as teacher notes on the board, personal notes, and their textbooks (Escalante, 2012). I realized this was the perfect marriage of the four domains of language and they were working in unison to develop language proficiency and content knowledge.

Alma Flor Ada states those four domains so succinctly:

Students need to hear the sounds of words and glean their meaning through attentive listening; they need to read and be read to extensively; they need to play with words, their multiple meanings, their sounds, and the rhythm that can be created with them; and they need the opportunity to develop their own voice in spoken and written form.

Alma Flor Ada (2003)

Students from both native English- and native Spanish-speaking backgrounds were interested enough in the development and outcome of their one-act plays that they often forgot they were even using two languages to communicate. They were motivated to fully participate in their groups.

Some students were very outgoing and extroverted, eager to act out their scenes while others were a bit more reserved, preferring to narrate or serve in smaller roles. Students, both ELLs and native English speakers, had the opportunity to choose roles that matched their individual personalities and talents. They were in a position to participate from within their comfort zones. At the same time, they had that freedom and opportunity to be creative and to bring their own background knowledge into the scene. They could choose to add humor—the students often laughed as they were discussing ideas with their groups. They were also able to display their unique talents. It provided a chance for them to share a bit of themselves with the others and to bring their own connections to the topic, which was very valuable in motivating them.

I watched how the students responded differently to various activities. As teachers we need to know that not all students will perceive all activities the same way, because each student has different interests. However, when I offered them a variety of activities and incorporated choices into those activities, it motivated them to become greater participants in the activities, and thus in the class. I started realizing that I needed to focus my energy on finding ways to motivate students.

Over the years, my dream to inspire teachers of English language learners became a reality as I started consulting in school districts across the state of Texas. Much of my work focused on equipping teachers to motivate ELLs through engaging literacy practices. My work with teachers and schools culminated in the writing and publication of this book. Its user-friendly format allows teachers to acquire a basic understanding of how to boost student motivation and participation

through tangible activities. As an educator, I feel there is no reason learning cannot be exciting, intriguing, and enjoyable for students every day. As my dad often reminded my siblings and me during our childhood, "You can't be bored until you're 99 and in a wheelchair." If my class is dull and lifeless, there is something I can do!

The desire to learn is ignited when students are captivated by their teachers, the content, relationships with peers, or any combination thereof. Attitudes toward academic topics radically change when ELLs enjoy the activities or methods through which they are learning. The classroom ambiance shifts from a stagnant, dull environment to one in which students are motivated and enjoying themselves. I wanted to provide a resource for teachers that makes it very easy to cultivate such a classroom, one relationship and one activity at a time. ***Motivation is the key to it all.***

Many aspects of teaching have a learning curve, and motivating English language learners through the avenues that are described in this book is no exception. Expect there to be bumps in the road, ups and downs, successes and frustrations; it may feel like you're on a roller coaster. Remind yourself that trying something new may create opportunities that improve the environment and outcomes in your classroom. Expect some activities to bomb (although sometimes only in your mind) the first time or two. The biggest mistake I have made, and one I think is common to many teachers, is setting strict time restraints for completing an activity the first few times I've tried it. Expect students to take about triple the time you initially anticipate. But remember, you've got this!

Let's get started >>>

Getting Started WITH MOTIVATING ELLS

Motivating ELLs means taking action that moves students to a level of participation where their language acquisition flourishes. There are many ways to categorize types of motivation, with two of the most common being extrinsic and intrinsic motivation. Extrinsic motivation includes reward systems that influence behavior, i.e., tokens, grades, and praise. Teachers often use extrinsic motivators to get students to behave well, participate in classroom activities, and complete assignments. Sometimes these may have a role in pushing ELLs to participate in activities that accelerate language acquisition. However, I have found that a lot of these reward systems are necessary only when the students are not interested in the material being discussed in class. There may be successful ways to work these reward systems into a classroom routine, but they will not be the focus of this book.

Instead I will be focusing on intrinsic motivation. This is the more powerful of the two because it comes from the students. It is something personal that moves them along, pushing them from within. To find it, we teachers need to ask what is it that is really motivating the students. Students may respond with:

"I want to learn this to be more knowledgeable, because I enjoy what I'm learning."

"I want to be a part of this learning experience because it seems fun to me."

"I want to be an integral part of this learning community because people care about me here."

"I want to participate in this activity because I know I'm learning when I do this."

"I want to learn because I want to improve myself."

"I want to improve my future possibilities."

We teachers can play a significant role in motivating students by digging deeper and figuring out what is interesting to them. "What do I know about these students that can help me engage them in this lesson?" Even if it's something small like, "Hey, I know that they enjoy eating tacos for breakfast," you can use it. Something as simple as tapping into musical preferences or information from their home countries (and tying these into our lessons) can go a long way toward increasing students' motivation. We can work with any little detail to build relationships with our students, achieve a more personal flow of communication, and foster an environment where English language learners are engaged and motivated to succeed.

>>> >>> English language learners are trying to figure out many facets of their lives all at once, and the classroom dynamics can seem overwhelming.

This can be a challenge because English language learners often come into a classroom that is linguistically and culturally foreign. For students who have attended school outside of the United States, the classroom environment, routines, and teaching methodologies in America are often vastly different from the procedures and expectations they have internalized from their previous educational experiences. They are not only navigating a completely new arrangement, but they're also navigating new relationships. They're trying to figure out what is acceptable to their new teachers while at the same time constructing their new social lives. English language learners are trying to figure out many facets of their lives all at once, and the classroom dynamics can seem overwhelming. Many times the first thing to suffer is their engagement in class, because when they know that a teacher is going to be okay with them being silent and not causing a ruckus in class, that's likely what they're going to do. With all the new social problems they're facing in school, the path of least resistance—just being silent in class—seems like an easy solution for many students.

This is unique to ELLs because students that were born in the United States generally have a common understanding of what is expected of them. There may be a great disparity between how grades work in their new country, seating arrangements, and campus size and orientation. English language learners may struggle with something as simple as how to get to class, how to navigate the campus, or what to do during the Pledge of Allegiance or school announcements. English language learners try to decipher what all this means, and one of the first instincts is for them to shut down. They just go internal, keep to themselves, and do whatever they have to do to keep the peace. This makes it difficult for ELLs to successfully navigate the process of acculturation, because they don't have a high number of interactions with their native English speaking peers.

There are many English language learners who do not understand that a formal education in their new country is absolutely vital to their future opportunities for employment. It's possible that in their home country, a formal education did not offer as many prospects as it does in the United States.

They may be unaware of what it costs to rent or buy a home and a car and raise a family. Alternatively, some ELLs may begin to comprehend the weight of their success or failure in terms of how much their parents sacrificed to bring them to a new country. The pressure to succeed, coupled with a lack of understanding of how they can succeed, can create the perfect storm of frustration and hopelessness. Educators who ask students caring but direct questions about their realities as they relate to their school lives can shine light in the darkness for students that are new to America.

However, English language learners in our classrooms are not only comprised of newcomers to this country. In fact, one of the largest grouping sub-populations of our ELLs are actually long-term ELLs, or those students that who have attended school in the U.S. for six or more years yet are still classified as ELLs. Many teachers struggle to meet the needs of these students. Characteristically, they are often fluent in conversational English, yet cannot be reclassified because they are unable to perform at expected levels on state assessments.

As teachers, we often also don't know what our English language learners expect from us or what they expect from their own roles as students. We need to understand where our ELLs are coming from, find out what they expect, and communicate what is expected of them. These are huge steps in developing student relationships. When we invest the time and effort in developing positive relationships with our students, particularly ELLs, we can understand their struggles and help them overcome hesitations to be fully participating members of the class and school.

Participation starts with the premise that we **can** get 100% engagement from our English language learners. As humans, we want our voices to be heard; that's true for speakers of any language, and it's true for even the quietest of English language learners. They want their ideas to be heard and their personalities to be seen in class. In this book, I tried to provide teachers the tools necessary to create opportunities for their students to speak and be heard. I have given real examples and real techniques for developing positive relationships with English language learners and amplifying their language

development. I included strategies that are easily applied in classrooms, that get students talking, using academic language, and engaging in meaningful conversations. The book illustrates concrete ways to integrate their students' ideas and personalities into the classroom. In addition, the structured nature of the activities can reduce teachers' anxiety about losing control of classroom management when providing students opportunities for interaction with each other by listening, speaking, reading, and writing.

*Motivating English Language Learner*s is an ideal resource for teachers who are new to teaching English language learners, as well as teachers who may have many years experience. It will help educators who are incorporating the four domains of language (listening, speaking, reading, and writing) and want to improve the way their students are engaged and motivated in class. It is also useful to anyone who supports teachers, such as teacher assistants, instructional coaches or mentors, and administrators.

Even though, as teachers, we are often obligated to cover a certain amount of content standards, we can help connect students' interests and background knowledge to any subject we teach. Even with the massive amount of content we are required to address in a school year, we have the liberty and the ability to connect themes and ideas to students' personal lives. Human characteristics and themes are timeless. Investigating and embracing student interests and connecting them to our own creativity as educators enables us to share our joy and passion for these subjects with our students!

I personally experienced this when I walked into a high school where the students in two different English classes were reading *The Day it Rained Cats* (Park, 2016). The main character is a young girl who discovers her grandmother has the ability to levitate objects and decides to dedicate herself to learning the skill. In the first classroom I observed, the teacher dove right into the story, assuming students were going to be as excited about it as she was. But they were completely disconnected. The concept of levitating objects seemed very abstract and far-removed from students' lived experiences. The teacher of the second class took the time to ask her students what they knew about their grandparents. What talents did their grandparents have that the students wished they could acquire or that they had acquired? The ELL students in this second class were motivated to read the text, because they wanted to find out how what they knew about their grandparents related to what this character was going to find out about her grandma.

With this small amount of digging, the teacher was able to hook students into the story. The level of motivation in the

classroom where the teacher **_had delved into the students' prior knowledge_** was vastly improved from the classroom whose teacher focused only on content. The process of accessing students' prior knowledge does not have to be complicated or lengthy. In fact, some of the most effective examples have come from quick warm-ups that teachers provide as a hook into the lesson at the beginning of class. For example, in an English class at another high school, the teacher linked classic poetry ("Ozymandias" by Percy Bysshe Shelley) to modern music ("Viva La Vida" by Coldplay) that students found fascinating.

Taking the time to access students' prior knowledge helps lower the affective filter for English language learners because it gives the students a chance to engage in something they know about—something that they feel connected to. Even the most obscure text can be tied into a student's background knowledge. This transforms learning by helping students who would not otherwise participate become interested. Of course, we not only want students to be interested in content, but we also want them to be internally challenged and inspired to move forward in language proficiency.

TWO KEYS
to Motivating English Language Learners ★

There are two vital non-negotiables to motivating ELLs:

- lowering the affective filter, and
- accessing prior knowledge.

These two concepts are woven throughout the activities in this book, so much so that the activities are really modes by which to accomplish these non-negotiables.

The first key, the affective filter, is an internal (emotional) barrier to receiving comprehensible input. Comprehensible input is a message that a student understands in a target language, whether visual, oral, or written (or a combination thereof). Students who are nervous or frightened or uncomfortable won't be able to hear or read those messages in a way they understand. When teachers ensure students feel comfortable and not stressed, they create environments that help lower English language learners' affective filters. When students have low affective filters and hear or read and understand messages in English, those messages result in language acquisition.

Sometimes, as teachers, we can have what we think is the most interesting lesson, but if our English language learners are nervous—whether it's because they don't know what to expect, the material is unfamiliar, or they are uncomfortable communicating with you or with their peers—they will not be motivated to participate fully in the lesson. If we can lower those barriers for our ELLs first, they are much more likely to engage in the content.

The second key, accessing prior knowledge, occurs when teachers take the time to find out how the students' personal lives or personal experiences relate to the lesson topic. As teachers, we help build this bridge for our students. One way we can do this is by asking a key question about how ELLs' prior experiences have affected their perception of the lesson topic. Tapping into something that students are either interested in, know something about, or have a previous experience with plays an important part in connecting students to the new knowledge they're going to be experiencing in class that day.

One of the most surprising findings in my doctoral work was how frequently students build on their shared school experiences. I explored ways to tap into this phenomena in order to link students' prior knowledge to new learning in my classroom. I worked with students to create a class chart to chronicle their experiences in our class, in other classes, around campus, and near the campus. I called this record of their experiences a schoologue (see pg 82). For example, fourth graders who had shared experiences in gym class with competitive team games connected those experiences to an understanding of two armies fighting each other in battle. How did the teams work together to win? How did the armies work as a team to overcome their opponent? Did the team rely on brute strength and numbers or strategic planning, spying, and outwitting the enemy?

Another example may come from a World Geography class where students have a common lunch hour. The teacher might capitalize on this by asking what English language learners ate the day before and how our geographical location in the world contributes to what we eat. How does food in the United States differ from that of their home country? Schoologues (see pg. 82) are an easy place to start for teachers, because whether students have shared school experiences from three days or three years, you can help them build on this background.

It is important to be deliberate about accessing prior knowledge everyday, because as teachers, we often don't know what experiences or ideas students possess until we ask. We should never assume that we know what their experiences are based on their country of origin, or their native language. We are often surprised at what they know or don't know and what interests they have. As teachers, we need to seek out the rich backgrounds and experiences our ELLs have to offer. (Moll et al, 1992)

What makes accessing prior knowledge so significant for ELLs is that it enables us to find input that will not just be comprehensible but also compelling. We don't know what's going to be interesting or engaging for students until we get to know them and access their background knowledge. To further shed light on this, Stephen Krashen wrote about the idea of compelling input (Krashen & Bland, 2014). Input doesn't just need to be comprehensible to kids; it also needs to be compelling. Compelling input should so intrigue the students - the material be so naturally engaging - that they will chase after it; that their minds crave more after the experience.

This book is organized into three broad categories:

Amplifying Language Development

Bridging Content Connections

Cultivating Relationships

These are the ABCs or the three pillars of building strong, motivated students in the classroom.

Amplifying Language Development refers to prioritizing students' oral and written self-expression. All students need to verbalize in order to internalize language, but this is particularly important for ELLs, who may not have ample opportunities to develop both social and academic language outside of their school days. Students' motivation increases when they are encouraged to express themselves and take risks with new language in a low-stress environment where mistakes are expected, students are not scolded, and the topics and activities are interesting to them.

Teachers are often the gatekeepers for this language output, as the atmospheres they develop and maintain determine the opportunities for such linguistic exchange.

Bridging Content Connections involves encouraging students to connect content and language objectives to meaningful experiences within their classroom community and beyond the school walls. Teachers who use creativity and engaging activities to actively pursue compelling and "outside-the-box" opportunities motivate their students to enjoy learning. Motivated students emerge as teachers base their practices on the idea that students have the ability to think, reason, and contribute to their school community not just memorize and regurgitate information. "Dialogues in which students have a personal stake and about which teacher and students have a mutual interest" fan the flame of motivation (Amato, 2010).

Finally, teaching is first and foremost about relationships. **Cultivating Relationships** with students is critical if we want to do more than just "water rocks." The water is the content, and it falls on rocks instead of fertile soil when students do not have a positive relationship with their teacher. Recall the old adage, "They don't care how much you know until they know how much you care." This is never more true than in teaching. According to Nieto (2015) teachers show how much they care for their students by the attention and time they devote to learning about students' experiences, interests, and backgrounds.

@ the world "STAAR" prep.

Nothing breaks my heart faster than asking a teacher midyear where her English language learners are from and discovering that she cannot even name the students' countries of origin. My husband and I now laugh about the time he told someone he was from Venezuela and the person replied, "Now what part of Mexico is that?" While simple geography would clarify that misconception, at the very least the person bothered to ask the question! How would you feel if you suddenly found yourself living in a foreign country, perhaps not even of your own choosing (which is often the case among newcomer ELLs), and after six months no one in your community had even bothered to find out where you were from? This little effort lays the initial groundwork for a positive relationship between teachers and English language learners. The crucial factor for students who move from defiant to compliant to motivated is often their positive relationship with their teacher.

The activities in this book give teachers a critical starting point from which to develop positive relationships with their students and their students' families. Each of the activities within these three categories helps English language learners lower their affective filters and provides an opportunity for the teacher to access their students' prior knowledge.

>>> >>> The crucial factor for students who move from defiant to compliant to motivated is often their positive relationship with their teacher.

Amplifying
LANGUAGE
DEVELOPMENT

We amplify language development for English language learners when we provide students opportunities to verbalize their thinking and to express ideas related to class content as they are learning it. This means giving students the chance to orally produce the academic vocabulary and work with it to find out how it has meaning for them.

When acquiring a language, it is essential to engage in all four language domains (Wright, 2016). Therefore, it is imperative that we provide daily opportunities for speaking, listening, reading, and writing in the classroom. When we foster an environment where discussions are valued and encouraged we create a classroom in which ELLs are willing, excited, and motivated to participate. In such an environment, students know their input is being acknowledged by their classmates and teachers, and that they are **authentically** contributing to the class.

Because ELLs come from different cultures, and the language is new to them, they can become extremely withdrawn or intimidated and reluctant to participate in classroom dialogue. They may be afraid to make mistakes. They may come from a more socially reserved culture. They may feel awkward. They may resist familiarizing themselves with their classmates or with the teacher. Some ELLs who are identified as long-term ELLs may require significant intervention to move them forward in English language proficiency.

Many ELLs will have limited opportunities to practice expressing their ideas in English outside of class, so the opportunities the teacher deliberately and intentionally creates may be their only opportunities to improve their language development. Amplifying language development enables ELLs to verbalize English, express content knowledge, and practice using words they need to be familiar with. This helps them be successful in the classroom, on assessments, and even in life.

How to AMPLIFY LANGUAGE DEVELOPMENT

- Encourage students to speak in complete sentences.

- Provide students with multiple opportunities to verbalize academic content and vocabulary.

- Create a language-rich environment where discussions are valued and encouraged.

- Repeat key vocabulary several times per lesson, and have students do the same. Challenge yourself to see how many times you can get students to say a word in class using a variety of stems.

If it doesn't happen at school, it might not happen.

The technological age means less speaking and more screen time (texting as opposed to talking to friends).

We can be surrounded by a language and never learn it.

As important as it is, amplifying language development is not without its challenges. Occasionally, teachers with the best intentions can hinder their English language learners' language development. For example, bilingual teachers often become comfortable using concurrent translation. At times it is easier to translate than to use other second-language learning strategies. Though translating the lesson into a student's native language may seem helpful in the short term, over time it undermines the student's motivation to learn English.

Another common challenge stems from the fact that teachers feel such pressure to cover an astronomical amount of material through their standards and through the pacing of their lessons that they may overlook activities that build language while teaching content, erroneously believing they just don't have sufficient minutes in the day. At the same time, teachers fret about how to increase academic language acquisition, scouring books for strategies to answer questions such as, "How can I get an English learner to produce this word and use it in meaningful ways? How many times can I get my ELLs to process this information while they're with me in this class period? How can I really maximize their language production for the short period of time that I have them?" This familiar struggle was paramount in my mind as I selected the strategies for this section, which is why they are very simple to implement and guaranteed to make amplifying language development an essential component of the classroom routine without it becoming an additional burden.

Our technological age presents another challenge, as there is a lot less speaking and a lot more screen time. Even socially, students are texting more than they are speaking with each other. If you sit in a cafeteria in a secondary school anywhere across the country, you'll see students texting or looking at something on their iPads instead of engaging in conversation with their friends at lunch. If that's happening in the lunchroom, it's also happening in the classroom.

Technology can also contribute to the phenomenon of students being surrounded by a language and never learning it: they are in an English-speaking school, but they are interacting on their devices in their native language. Unfortunately, this problem may occur even when students are not using technology. Students can sit all day in a classroom where the language

is English (the language they need to be learning), but they are not acquiring it because their affective filters are high and we may not be creating environments that are motivating enough for them to take part in the academic conversations.

English language learners must have opportunities to talk in every class, every day. Sometimes they are only motivated to participate in these conversations when we show them that their ideas really matter; that we, as teachers, are not the only sources of knowledge in the classroom (Freire, 1998). I have won over resistant students by showing them that their voices are heard, and that the subject matter can be enjoyable. When their ideas became part of the lesson, they enjoyed the positive attention.

>>> >>> As I have grown in my capacity as a teacher, I have come to realize how important it is for my classroom to provide speaking and listening opportunities. Saying their ideas aloud, especially if they have written them down first, helps them identify weaknesses in their arguments. I will often hear students reading what they wrote and then backtracking with a 'wait, that doesn't make sense' or their partner pointing out that they can add onto their thought with something. This also has the added benefit of helping their writing, because they hear it read aloud and can spot mistakes more easily when they hear them.

Katherine Perry,
Middle School Teacher of the Year, 2017

In order to allow students' voices to be heard, we need to be consistent and intentional about structuring the time and the language that students are using for their interactions. It is possible that your classroom might be the first place a student has been held accountable for processing content orally with their classmates. This is why it is essential that we create environments in which students feel comfortable speaking with one another and are willing to contribute whether it is a conversation between two students, among a small group, or with the entire class. When students are given a chance to talk to one another—and given ways to begin that conversation, such as sentence stems or particular words and academic vocabulary—they are less intimidated. Over time, participation in conversations like these make English language learners more comfortable and lower their affective filters, making them more motivated to participate in classroom activities.

HELPFUL HINTS To get your students verbalizing and mobilizing

- Plan 2-5 minute blocks throughout your lessons during which students can engage in structured conversation. This may take 5-10 minutes when it is new.

- Consider timing yourself in order to assess the balance of teacher talk and student talk.

- Display 2-3 simple sentence stems that students can access.

- Randomly select which student starts the student-student conversation.

- Be patient. It takes time and consistency.

- Give genuine praise and feedback for students' comments.

- Enhance listening skills by allowing students to respond to peers.

- Hold students accountable for contributing, supporting them as needed.

MOVE & TALK

We are physical beings, and our bodies were made to move. Providing times in which students can actually get up out of their seats and move around is essential to motivation. Many times there is little to no physical movement during a lesson, and yet research shows that physical movement, or linking the physical with the mental, is an important way to make content connections (Asher, 1969). Language is amplified when movement is paired with interaction.

When ELLs are given a chance to interact with different speakers—both other ELLs and native English peers—they hear a variety of language. They hear different accents and pronunciations. They hear different thoughts and manners of expression. They hear different sentence styles and sentence structures. When they interact with their peers while incorporating movement, they keep their minds engaged, but they also add to their linguistic repertoire because they see different models from their peers. In comparison, students who do not have opportunities to move and talk only hear from the teacher and the limited number of peers who are in close proximity.

Michael Long talks about a concept called "negotiated input" (1983). It refers to the event that occurs when two persons are speaking—for example a native-English speaking student and an English learner—and one speaker doesn't understand something. The other tends to clarify it. The interactive nature of the input when students are moving and talking allows the English learner to acquire more language.

This concept is closely related to the Language Experience Approach (Nessel & Dixon, 2008). It's why the first part of language experience approach is so successful, because the students are talking about this shared experience and contributing back and forth in their own languages, and negotiating meaning for each other.

Gallery Walk & T[...]

DESCRIPTION Students assem[...] m
where a visual or text is posted [...] ps,
students engage in a discussio[...] their
thoughts using complete sente[...] as
when to rotate and how many [...] oom
management needs.

Based on "lucky Red Envelope" I can infer "this person beliefs in superstition"

DIRECTIONS

1. Select a text that can be separated [...] s.

2. Post appropriate response stems alongside the question(s). You may want to provide both simple and more complex stems to support variations in English language proficiency.

3. Divide the text into a specific number of short, digestible pieces, being mindful of what students can accomplish in three to five minutes.

4. Compose at least one essential question that relates to each section of text selected and/or visual posted.

5. Number the texts and visuals, and display them around the room.

6. Have students write down the numbers that will correspond to each station.

7. Organize students into pairs or triads.

8. Assign each pair/triad to a numbered station. Consider assigning roles to students.

9. Explain the rotation process to students. Their beginning position can be random or assigned.

10. Remind students of the expectations related to accountable talk during stations. If necessary, model both examples and non-examples of desired behaviors.

11. Have students discuss the text selection or visual, write down their response(s) to the question(s), and rotate to the next station on your direction.

12. Once the activity concludes and students have returned to their seats, randomly choose members of the class to share their responses.

EXAMPLES

Elementary:

Essential question:
What is one way you can describe this picture using a fraction or fractions?

Stems:
I notice that ____ frogs are/have ____.

____ out of ____ frogs are ____.

The fraction representing this picture would be __/__.

Secondary:

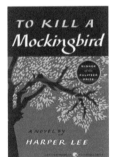

Text: *To Kill a Mockingbird*
Essential question: Throughout the novel, several different characters feel angry. Who do you think handles it best? Why?

Stems:
In chapter ___, (character) feels angry because ____. I agree with how he/she responds to that anger because ____.

(Character) handled their anger the best because _____. I agree with how he/she handled it because ____.

Other examples:

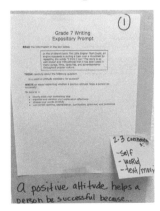

Right: Students learn how to start an essay by verbalizing and practicing with partners around the room.

Left: Students visit science vocabulary around the room.

Roving Paragraph Frames

DESCRIPTION Roving Paragraph Frames is an activity that combines listening, speaking, reading, and writing in an interactive format to benefit all learners. Students engage in a series of short conversations, each of which culminates in the creation of a new sentence. The collection of sentences eventually forms a paragraph. This strategy can be used as a warm-up activity, a transition midway through a class period, or as closure to review the day's concepts and learning.

DIRECTIONS

1. Give students a sentence stem to begin the activity. Allow students time to think and then time to write their completed stems on their paper.

2. Ask the students to stand up with their paper and pencils when they have completed the written sentence.

3. Have the students "rove" around the room and find a partner.

4. Ask students to read their writing to one another. The first person reads his or her complete sentence, stem and all. The second person listens, and then reads his or her complete sentence.

5. The partners then collaborate to write a new sentence that begins with a new stem. They can either "borrow or steal" each other's responses if they were different, or they can just create a fresh sentence. Once sentence number two is complete, partners raise their hands or stand back to back. The key here is to incorporate total response signals to indicate to the teacher that the task is complete. Now they are ready to rove again!

6. Have the students find new partners and repeat the entire process with the second partner. It is crucial to instruct students to take turns reading everything they have written so far and listening to each other's sentences. This validates student responses and encourages the use of listening and speaking skills. After reading individual sentences, students write a third sentence with another stem.

7. To conclude, have students repeat the process one last time, roving to find their final partners. Once each partner reads his or her individual sentences aloud, ask students to write the final sentence using the last stem. At this point, each student should have a well-constructed paragraph in hand, complete with transitions and complete thoughts recorded in academic English.

EXAMPLES

Elementary:
Physical characteristics that help turtles survive include…
Furthermore…
In addition…
Finally…

Secondary:
Understanding the Bill of Rights is essential for all citizens because…
In addition…
Considering that…
Finally…

Walking Worksheets

DESCRIPTION This activity breaks up the monotony of sitting down to complete meaningful practice by having students locate components of the worksheet throughout the room. By adding the elements of choice and movement, the teacher increases both the level of engagement and the amount of information retained.

DIRECTIONS

1. Select an unused worksheet or a set of unanswered test questions.

2. Cut the worksheet or test section into individual items.

3. Tape each section around the room in a different location (not necessarily in order).

4. Have students set up their journals or paper on a clipboard.

5. Differentiation: Pair struggling students with more advanced students to support them. Model how students should work together to solve the problem and show evidence of their process. Beginner ELLs may copy a sentence from the text or look for a word and add a quick illustration. Pre-K and kindergarten students can engage in oral conversation or matching words with pictures and realia with a partner at each station.

6. Roam around the room supporting students and encouraging them to spend an estimated number of minutes on each problem. Consider using a timer with a few minutes built in at the end to revisit any unfinished stations.

7. Randomly select students to answer and model how they solved the problems.

EXAMPLES

Teacher models how to set up and works through a sample.

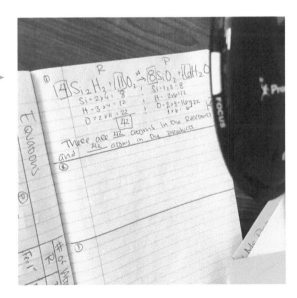

Biology students practice balancing equations.

Students read and respond to text selections using provided stems.

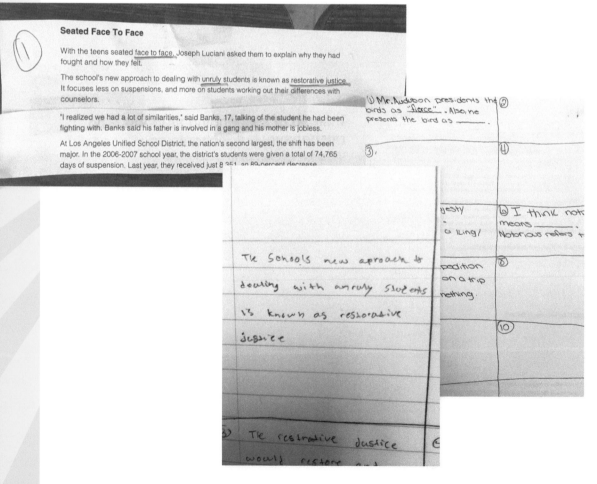

ROLE PLAY

Role play provides an opportunity to get students to put themselves in the position of a character or a concept that the content addresses. Options range from one-act plays to Reader's Theater to improvisations, such as having students take on the roles of experts and novices on a given topic. Students may even take on the roles of inanimate objects or content concepts (for example, the perspective of a raindrop going through the water cycle!).

ELLs in particular enjoy role playing because the affective filter is lowered when students are putting themselves in the place of someone or something else. As they consider how that person or object would think or talk, they focus more on the content and the process, and less on themselves as individuals.

Getting into character and experimenting with different voices and circumstances can create this meaningful purpose for students. Ladousse asserts that "role play is one of a whole gamut of communicative techniques which develops fluency in language students, which promotes interaction in the classroom, and which increases motivation" (2004, p.24). In addition, Ladousse points out that role play encourages peer learning and sharing of responsibility for learning between teacher and student. He suggested role play to be "perhaps the most flexible technique in the range" of communicative techniques, and noted that teachers who promote role play with suitable and effective activities can meet an infinite variety of learner needs. Role playing helps individuals become more flexible and develop a sense of mastery in many situations. It allows language learners to experience situations in which they will use the language and then draw from these linguistic skills when needed.

>>> >>> Language needs to be used in real situations, for authentic and meaningful purposes, and in a variety of circumstances.

Alma Flor Ada, 2003

>>> >>> During role play, students are given the opportunity to negotiate language with peers. The teacher decides when and when not to intervene with students, judging when it would be beneficial to allow students to work through language options and content decisions together without adult redirection.

Escalante, 2012

T-Chart, Pair, Defend

DESCRIPTION The ability to express and defend more than one position on a given issue is one of the most crucial skills teachers can impart to their students. During this task, students are guided through the process of talking and writing from differing perspectives. Through shared writing and then individual reflection, students form their own opinions and strengthen their individual voices.

DIRECTIONS

1. Discuss key ideas and academic vocabulary from the text. (Reference ideas from "Start With a Spark" [see pg. 58] activity to hook students.)

2. Model how to set up a T-chart, providing sentence stems that encourage students' use of vocabulary.

3. Allow students time to brainstorm and write down ideas from their perspectives. Consider dividing the class so that both sides are well represented.

4. Facilitate a classroom debate-style dialogue in which students role-play.

5. Follow up the structured debate with time for writing final thoughts or new ideas students glean from the discussion.

EXAMPLE

You are Kenny from *The Watsons Go to Birmingham*. Read Chapter 4: "Froze-Up Southern Folks." Consider how the cold weather affects Kenny, his mother, his siblings, and the bullies. Should he defend himself (retaliate) against Larry Dunn?

VOCABULARY: frostbite, dangerous, gloves, snow pants, coat, bullies, whining, complaining, burying, punching, humor

Kenny should defend himself, because…	Kenny should not defend himself, because…
The cold weather is beneficial in that…	The cold weather is detrimental in that…
Kenny's mom should wrap the kids in many layers of clothing, because…	Kenny's mom should not wrap the kids in so many layers, because…

Script Writers

DESCRIPTION Students amplify their language development and showcase their creativity by writing short plays with classmates. Teachers should encourage students to use key vocabulary from the content and/or language objective and mentor texts and also encourage students to approach the task with imagination. Teachers may suggest that students create simple props or backdrops to enhance their performances or that they give voice to inanimate objects to offer unique perspectives. For purposes of differentiation, beginners may have roles with simple language and gestures while more advanced speakers could be expected to memorize lines to perform for the class.

Note: Assuming they have practice time, even a newcomer can practice one or two simple statements

DIRECTIONS

1. Review the content and/or language objective and vocabulary students will be asked to use in their one-act plays.

2. Model with students how characters can be given a voice while also integrating vocabulary. Support this new learning with mentor Readers' Theater texts (script forms of a written text).

3. Specify how many characters, lines, and vocabulary terms each group is required to include in their play.

4. Allow time for each group to work on their play. Rotate through groups to support progress.

5. Provide time for students to edit their plays as well as other groups' plays, as time permits. You may want to model specific revisions or editing strategies.

6. Give students time to have a dress rehearsal with any props or backdrops they choose.

7. Students may choose to record and show the class their recorded play or enjoy providing a live performance.

8. Consider using a rubric to measure student success. If a rubric is created, share it with the students at the beginning of the project so they know exactly what to work toward.

EXAMPLES

Elementary:

Fourth graders depict a scene in Texas history, such as a battle scene or the moment a group of pioneers arrives to establish a new settlement.

Predators and prey voice how they will capture or be captured and how their adaptations will affect a scenario in nature.

Secondary:

Former slaves discuss their route to freedom and the challenges they encountered along the way.

Improv Read-Aloud

DESCRIPTION During this exercise, students act out a story silently while the teacher or another student reads it aloud. This motivates ELLs to actively listen to a more advanced speaker and enjoy engaging more fully in the story.

DIRECTIONS

Prior to reading, have each set of partners invent gestures for two or three words from the chosen text to teach the class. After the class has practiced all gestures for academic vocabulary words, the teacher (or student) slowly reads the text aloud with intonation, pausing intentionally on keywords to allow students to gesture. You may choose to incorporate a little friendly competition by extending a challenge to two sides of the class. Which side can act out the reading most enthusiastically? Which side remembers the most gestures as the text is being read? Add physical movement for longer texts by having students change positions around the room after each paragraph or page. Knock on a desk to signal rotation. This works well when each student has a copy of the text. The text may also be a poem or song displayed on a screen. You may choose to hand out index cards with key words from the text written on them. Students can hold them up in the air when they hear the word read aloud.

EXAMPLE

Excerpt from *Sometimes* by Hugo Ibarra & John Seidlitz
Gesture words: *money, nothing, feeling*

My dad was still sending us money *every week and all we had to do was go to a local store to get it. Until one day the cashier told Mom that* nothing *had come for us that week. I had the* feeling *that something was not OK.*

MUSIC

Music is so important to human beings. Every culture and every generation has music that is appealing and that awakens the spirit. Students come to our classes with different passions about music. You'll be hard-pressed to find someone who doesn't enjoy some kind of music, even if it varies greatly from one student to another. You'll notice that, from Pre-K through 12th grade, students are always singing something or humming a tune. If they hear a song, they're repeating it, whether they're two-year-olds or adults. When you tap into that musical interest with your students, you can apply it in your lessons and use it to motivate them to learn the content and be an active part of the class.

The repetitive nature of music lends itself to language acquisition. In particular, one of the advantageous features of a chorus is that it is repeated throughout the song. When that chorus includes academic vocabulary words, students can connect those words to their meanings or something they have done in class. Likewise, teachers can embed the definitions, or the ideas behind those words, in the song itself. The repetitive nature of music is also useful linguistically, because repetition is key in solidifying those words, language structures, and ideas in your long-term memory.

In this way, music can help students acquire not only vocabulary but content knowledge and language structures. The phrases and structures they hear can help them develop their understanding of English—in both meaning and form. The benefit to using music is also found in its appeal to students of different proficiency levels in English. Beginners, for example, can enjoy music for its rhythm and its ability to help them understand basic vocabulary. Students who are more advanced in English might come in already knowing lyrics to a song but not really understanding the meaning. As their comprehension of the lyrics increases, they can apply that knowledge to the words they're already familiar singing. For students at all proficiency levels, the poetic devices of the songs can be analyzed and used to help the students understand many aspects of the language.

Music is also appealing because of its universally meaningful nature and ability to evoke human emotion. Besides its appeal, another important aspect to consider is that music breaks down barriers among those who share an interest in a particular type of music. Tapping into my students' different musical interests and pulling music from different cultures and genres ensures that I am providing a link to meaningful language practice opportunity for my students. If I get to know what my students' musical interests are, I can connect

these interests to content and use them as a basis for learning. Furthermore, the discourse features of songs tend to have that stuck-in-your-head idea (technically called involuntary musical imagery) that you end up thinking about long after you finish actually listening to or singing the song.

To find music your class will find engaging, speak to students outside of school, and ask them, "What kind of songs are popular now with your friends? Are there any that have clean lyrics that would be appropriate to share with students in class?" When students share music with me, I make a playlist on my phone that I can then share in class. They might be surprised that you, as a person of a different generation and perhaps culture, have actually taken the time to invest in their music, something they may not have experienced in the past.

Music is also a uniquely effective medium for reducing anxiety and self-consciousness. This is particularly true for second-language learners, and it's a phenomenon I experienced personally when I was learning a second language. I would be remiss if I didn't credit a good deal of my Spanish language development to Enrique Iglesias and Ana Gabriel, as well as the hymns we sang at a Spanish congregation where I

attended services for a year. I know firsthand how music motivated and enhanced my own second-language acquisition. I'll never forget this line from one of the songs that I used to sing at church:

Si no hubiera sido por el Señor,
Mi alma se hubiera perdido,
Si no hubiera sido por el Señor.

As a beginner Spanish speaker, I understood the general message of this simple song. As a more advanced speaker, I appreciated it in a new way: it helped me learn language form and in turn allowed me to sound more like a native speaker. I struggled with the past imperfect tense of Spanish before I heard and sang this song over and over until it stuck and became a part of the way I spoke in Spanish. I became comfortable using the stem "Si no hubiera sido por…" (*If it had not been for…*) and integrating it into social conversations as well as classroom settings. I could tell my native Spanish-speaking roommate from Guatemala, "Si no hubiera sido por tu ayuda, no hubiera pasado la clase." (*If it had not been for you, I would not have passed the class.*) I could tell a professor, "Si no hubiera sido por tu clase, no hubiera aprendido español." (*If it had not been for your class, I would not have learned Spanish.*)

>>> >>> ELLs not only enjoy music for its rhythm and personal appeal, but they are simultaneously learning language structure, vocabulary, expressions, phrasing, and idioms. This amplifies their language development, both socially and academically, in a unique way that spoken language does not.
Murphey, 1990

Song Writers

DESCRIPTION Students use the tune to a popular song to create lyrics that relate to the content objective and include meaningful vocabulary. They share with the class by singing as a team, a class, or posting online.

DIRECTIONS

1. Listen to the original lyrics of a popular song or chant with which students are familiar.

2. Sing the song or chorus several times with students.

3. Present students with meaningful vocabulary from the content objective and/or lesson.

4. Model how students can create their own lyrics as they include ideas, definitions, and vocabulary terms that will help them learn and remember the objective. (Consider breaking up a long vocabulary list by assigning certain terms to each group.)

5. Have students share their new lyrics with the class through the format of their choice: chart paper, smart board, screen, or an app such as ChatterPix.

EXAMPLES

Sample content objective:

5th grade TEKS:
Writing/Persuasive Texts: Students write **persuasive** texts to **influence the attitudes or actions** of a specific **audience** on specific issues.

5.19A: Students are expected to write persuasive essays for appropriate **audiences** that **establish a position** and include sound reasoning, detailed and **relevant evidence,** and consideration of alternatives.

Original Song: from "Firework" by Katy Perry	**Adapted Lyrics**
'Cause baby you're a firework	'Cause **persuasive** is a **writing genre**
Come and show 'em what you're worth	You **convince your audience** to do something
Make 'em go "oh, oh, oh!"	Make 'em go **"I'll do that!"**
As you shoot across the sky-y-y	As you **influence their actions and attitudes**
Baby you're a firework	Make sure that you **establish a position**
Come and let your colors burst	Using **reasoning and relevant evidence**
Make 'em go "oh, oh, oh!"	Make 'em go **"I'll do that!"**
You're gonna leave 'em falling down down down	You're gonna leave 'em **convinced, convinced!**

Song Search

DESCRIPTION There is an immense wealth of educational lyrics available on the Internet (most of which are free, making teachers everywhere smile). This blessing can also be a curse, as teachers find themselves spending precious planning time scouring the internet for those songs, chants, and short videos most worthy of sharing with students. In this activity, students become the curators of academic content. With specific directions, academic vocabulary to look for, and a structured timeframe to guide them, students can become teachers as they discover songs that will help them understand and remember content. Student motivation increases as they are given the opportunity to select and introduce their classmates to songs that would otherwise have been overlooked. This transfer of responsibility motivates students to take on a teaching role.

DIRECTIONS

Present students with a clear learning objective that incorporates key academic vocabulary. Delineate clear parameters for the time they will have to complete the task, the maximum length of media allowed, as well as terms they should use to help refine their search..

EXAMPLE

Learning objective: We will learn about the advantages and disadvantages of credit cards versus debit cards.

Within this objective, the teacher elicits background knowledge. What do the words advantage and disadvantage mean? What is another way to say that? (Positive/negative, pros/cons, good/bad, etc.) What about credit and debit cards? What do students already know about these?

Length: The song or short lesson should be four minutes or less.

Time: You will have 20 minutes to research and choose a song to present to the class.

Content: The song must include these terms: *advantage/disadvantage* (or synonyms), *credit, debit*

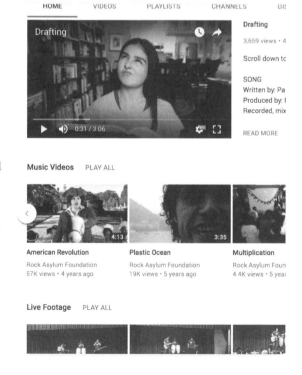

Music Memory

DESCRIPTION Music has long been a tool used by teachers to help students to memorize and remember content. Students sing songs that include all of the states, the presidents in order of term of office, hierarchies, etc. Short jingles can lock in information as well. The use of song with Dictado can enrich the writing experience as well. See Dr. Kathy Escamilla's article (Escamilla et al., 2009) on how to use this technique.

DIRECTIONS

Choose a song or chant that incorporates specific vocabulary from the learning objective. Create (or have students create) gestures to accompany key terms. Sing, and have students stand up and repeat each line as they use the appropriate gestures. Be expressive (or extremely silly—your call), and students will feed off your energy! Consider friendly competition between two or three groups in class to see who can deliver the best performance.

Note: It is important to keep songs or chants simple, especially at the beginning. Although it can be tempting to choose a song that includes abundant, rich vocabulary and complex phrasing in an effort to maximize the time and content, it is not advisable. If necessary, make up a simple song yourself with two to three lines (see example below) that include a few key vocabulary terms and concepts instead of choosing complicated lyrics from another source.

EXAMPLES

Here is a simple song that introduces young bilingual students to the body parts of a turtle.
caparazón (turtle shell), *vértebra* (vertebra), *plastrón* (underbelly plate), *cuello retractil* (retractable neck)

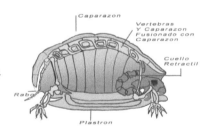

Tortugas, Tortugas, tienen caparazón Tortugas, Tortugas, tienen vértebra, Tortugas, Tortugas, tienen un plastrón Y un cuello retractil!	*English translation:* Turtles, Turtles, have a shell Turtles, Turtles, have vertebra Turtles, Turtles, have a plastron And a retractable neck!

The teacher should add a few simple gestures to accompany each body part and a few exaggerated high notes slightly off key to add some humor. When I used this strategy recently, I heard students singing this song on their own for the remainder of the week after just a few minutes in class!

B Bridging

CONTENT CONNECTIONS

Content that we address as teachers is dear to us; we are passionate about it. We may have spent years training to teach a certain subject matter or endured teaching other subjects until we landed a position that was just right for our interests and backgrounds. Because of our passion, we might even assume that the content will be just as interesting to the students. However, when students don't have the same background information or interests that teachers have, both parties can experience frustration and disappointment.

>>>>>> We can ignite that *chispa*, that spark, and pull them into the lesson.

Not only do students have different levels of background knowledge, but the language barrier adds a layer of complexity with ELLs. Fortunately, there are many ways in which we can make those content connections for students. We can build the bridges that connect background knowledge and new academic content. We can ignite that *chispa*, that spark, and pull them into the lesson.

There are often simple things we can do to help students connect even the most abstract idea to something that is personal to them. For example, reading a text about cells and the function of the kidneys and discussing diabetes may have no interest for students if they lack the background knowledge or any personal experience related to the topic. However, when Mrs. Farell (a biology teacher that I was coaching) shared her personal struggle with childhood diabetes with her high school students, she was able to explain how this challenge motivated her to learn about her body in order to live a healthy life. That newfound interest in turn led her to study biology in college and ultimately become a science teacher. After this introduction, she showed students the insulin pump connected to her beltloop. Jaws dropped. The students' would never have related diabetes to a young, athletic woman. She then posed a few key questions for her students to ponder: "Do you know someone with diabetes? How does it affect their lifestyle? If you had diabetes, how would it affect your lunch in the cafeteria or the extracurricular activities you could participate in?"

Now imagine a room full of high school football players in an algebra class. What do they care about linear equations? Suddenly they recognize a football play from their last home game on the screen that their teacher has just displayed. The lines that represent players' moves can be represented by linear equations. She just built a bridge between their background knowledge (and interests) and the content.

This bridge between content and students is beneficial for all learners but absolutely vital for English language learners. Information that is memorized in isolation may only be retained temporarily as opposed to being stored more permanently in long-term memory. That is why students can "cram" for a Friday quiz over the steps of mitosis, ace the test, and return to class Monday with little to no recollection of what they had studied. If what is being learned lacks relevancy or connection to prior learning (even students' own lives), it is unlikely to be retained. As a result, students will be unable to apply the previously taught information to new learning.

ELLs need a reason to be involved in the lesson. Tapping into these prior experiences by asking them questions they can relate to, and encouraging them to participate in meaningful conversations that will launch the lesson, will give them a reason to become personally invested. If a teacher can tap into a connection for students and capture their attention and interest, the likelihood of students fully participating in the classroom activities skyrockets.

Making explicit connections between the content being taught and the specific standards being targeted is essential for English language learners. Native English-speaking teachers have a bank of knowledge and experiences that are tied to information we have acquired from growing up in this country. Still, the United States is quite large and culturally diverse, even among native English speakers. That's why taking time to clarify any unfamiliar or ambiguous terms can benefit all students, not just those at the beginning stages of English proficiency. Both beginning ELLs and those of intermediate proficiency experience the inevitable struggle and frustration of being limited in their ability to communicate effectively. Because of this, it can take quite a bit of effort on the part of the teacher to determine what these students already know, in terms of both content and culture.

Keep in mind that it is not only our beginners, but also long-term ELLs that face their own set of challenges when it comes to bridging content connections. Long-term ELLs may have missed important concept development or content knowledge in their early years in school due to limited English proficiency. As older students, their English language proficiency is at a level where they can participate meaningfully in RtI interventions appropriate to their needs. Their lack of academic success is likely due to this gap in concept development or content knowledge rather than linguistic difficulties. With these students it is particularly important to bridge content connections.

CHOICES & STUDENT AUTONOMY

STRATEGIC USE OF NATIVE LANGUAGE

Have native-language peers briefly describe assignments or relay information between student and teacher.

Pair students so that the more proficient student is challenged to relay the lesson's goal.

Avoid concurrent translation, as it can hinder language development.

Utilize technology for translation purposes to allow participation by students who may not have native-language peers.

GET TO KNOW YOUR STUDENTS

Welcome from all linguistic, cultural, and socioeconomic backgrounds.

Move beyond the school walls (i.e., home visits, stores, eateries).

Invite students to bring in pictures or artifacts.

Ask students to create posters or graphic organizers that represent themselves and give the teacher insight to their lives.

When we are planning a vacation, why do we weigh the options? When we are looking at possible job opportunities, why do we consider alternatives? We enjoy having choices. What is true for adults is also true for students. Given choices, students are more likely to be motivated.

Many students wish for greater autonomy in the school setting. Giving students as many content-related choices as possible can be very valuable for them. This is particularly true for newcomers, who may be hesitant, reluctant, or even outright angry about their new reality. When giving students choices, we acknowledge that they also enjoy making decisions. In doing so, we communicate that we trust them to do so wisely. Simple choices can include which group of peers to work with, which text to read first, or a gallery walk in which they choose the order of practice problems. Students practice responsible behavior while making choices and learning content. From these simple choices, teachers can encourage deeper conversations about the application of knowledge with open-ended questioning. Students are often more motivated in conversations by questions that start with, "How would you..." or "Why do you think..." than questions starting with "What," "When," or "Who."

Teachers who genuinely listen to and learn from their students exemplify the reciprocal nature of teaching and learning which acknowledges students' voices and motivates them to engage further in the class and with the content. A simple example of the application of this idea in class could be to ask students questions related to a lesson's main objective, such as the following:

Why are we learning this?

How would I compare this to something else I've learned?

How do we know _____ is true?

How does this apply to my life?

How does this relate to what we will learn next?

While it is culturally acceptable for native English speakers to advocate for themselves, some ELLs may not have experienced this same norm. Students who come from other cultures and countries might not know what is acceptable, and they may hesitate to voice their personal opinions or thoughts. They may worry about how their opinions or ideas will be received or interpreted. Even long-term ELLs often struggle with self-advocacy because of the experience of being overlooked and 'stuck' in the system. As teachers provide students opportunities to exercise choice and autonomy in class, ELLs become more and more comfortable expressing their ideas.

ELLs may be coming from cultures where, at least at school, they're not accustomed to making choices about their learning. Students are more apt to produce output or partake in an activity if they have developed the self-confidence to think, "This is a choice that I know I'm capable of making." Overall ownership of learning is increased with more autonomy and participation. Additionally, choices lower the affective filter by creating that stress-free envi-

ronment where student preferences are validated, leading students to think, "My opinion is accepted, and I can partake in this activity."

Even beginner ELLs are capable of expressing preferences when allowed to do so non-linguistically. While they might not yet be comfortable verbalizing their thoughts and their opinions in English, students in the earliest stages of acquisition are able to point to one of three texts they want to read or choose between images that represent each of those texts. Providing this simple option will go a long way in fostering autonomy and student choice.

I, myself, learned an important lesson about giving students choices while teaching fourth grade. As I surveyed the room of cooperative learning groups, I was mentally high-fiving myself for creating such an engaged group of learners. A moment later, an inquisitive young student came over to me and said, "This group work is all fine and nice, but when do we get the worksheets?" I was baffled. Wasn't I just congratulating myself for avoiding boring worksheets in favor of more interactive learning? My first reply was, "Well, honey, I'm not really a worksheet-y kind of teacher." But after some reflection I realized, maybe he was a worksheet-y kind of student. He enjoyed the challenge of successfully completing a worksheet and having a type of closure and a grade that he achieved individually. The next day, and occasionally from then on, I offered him a worksheet instead of group work. Sometimes he took me up on the option, and sometimes he didn't. But that choice made all the difference in his attitude and actions.

Few adults are enticed into teaching with hopes of being told what to teach and how to teach it every minute of every school day. The enthusiasm with which most teachers enter the field quickly evaporates when we are told what material to cover, when to cover it, and how to evaluate students' performance with little room for choice or creativity. Perhaps as teachers we don't always realize that the same thing holds true for students: deprive them of self-determination, and you have likely deprived them of motivation. If learning is a matter of following orders, students simply will not take to it in the way they would if they had some say about what they were doing.

The seminal research of Kohn (1993) includes numerous surveys of American schools that reveal how rarely students are invited to become active participants in their own education. Schooling is typically about bestowing lessons on children, not working with them to learn the material. An array of punishments and rewards is often used to enforce compliance to an agenda that students rarely have any opportunity to influence.

Conversely, when students are given an opportunity to collaborate with teachers and make decisions about curriculum and grades they learn valuable lessons in class rather than just remembering information for a short period of time in order to pass a test. Collaborative learning that allows students to make reasonable choices has also been referred to as "participatory language teaching" (Auerbach, 2000). Ideally, the classroom setting would be one that exudes mutual respect and fosters positive relationships, and one in which everyone teaches and everyone learns.

Teachers may not always have the discretion to let students participate in deciding what topic to study. But even when compelled to teach a certain lesson, a teacher might open up a discussion in which members of the class try to figure out together why someone thought the subject was important enough to be required. The next step would be to connect that topic to students' real-world concerns and interests. Even when students are excluded for one reason or another from the selection of the subject matter, there is still room to give them choices about the specific questions or areas to explore within a general topic. Even within strict subject-matter parameters, teachers can offer choices in activities that allow students to choose the most meaningful ways in which they interact with the material and each other. A teacher might begin any unit, for example, by inviting students to discuss what they already know about the subject and what they would like to investigate.

ACCESSING STUDENTS' PRIOR KNOWLEDGE
Ask relevant questions to discover what students already know about the content or about a theme within the topic.
Have peers explain the concept to each other in their native language.
Utilize meaningful visuals as a springboard for students to discuss what they already know.
Consider incorporating historical or cultural references that are relevant to students (alliteration or tongue-twisters in other languages).

Build a Bowl

DESCRIPTION Build a Bowl allows student choice while connecting to creativity. Based on ideas from Carol Ann Tomlinson (2014), students are given a choice of text, a writing topic, and a visual representation to highlight key passages or quotes from a chosen genre. At any given point in a unit of study, students can build on what they already know by choosing from the bowl of ideas. This activity encourages students to revisit text when they are completing sentence stems. Technology can easily be integrated into the visual representation choices. This activity works well for any content area (math, science, etc.), as students can quote textbooks or anchor charts in the classroom.

DIRECTIONS

Model for students how to quote text (with accurate citations, if applicable).

TEXT	STEMS	VISUAL REPRESENTATION	CONTEMPORARY or PERSONAL APPLICATION
Quote 1	*This quote reveals...*	Create an ad for...	
Quote 2	*Based on this text I can infer...*	Find or draw a picture that represents the meaning of the word...	
Quote 3	*According to this text...*	Develop an action image with dialogue that shows...	

EXAMPLES

Elementary: The Little Red Hen

Quote	Stem	Visual Representation	Contemporary or Personal Application
"So the little red hen brought the wheat to the mill all by herself, ground the wheat into flour, and carried the heavy sack of flour back to the farm."	*Based on this text, I can infer that the little red hen was a hard worker. She was determined to get a bag of flour made out of the wheat even if no one was willing to help her.*	Employment ad: Looking for hard-working employees who are willing to learn all aspects of production from harvesting to baking. Must be willing to be trained for all skills. Compensation will reflect often-isolated working conditions.	I help my mom in the kitchen even though my brother and sister just want to play. Anyway, I get to sample all the food first (even the dough!), and they get what's leftover.

Secondary: **To Kill a Mockingbird**

Quote

"First of all," he said, "if you can learn a simple trick, Scout, you'll get along a lot better with all kinds of folks. You never really understand a person until you consider things from his point of view… until you climb into his skin and walk around in it." (Atticus)

Stem

This quote reveals how Atticus feels about compassion being based on empathy. He explains to his children how essential it is to be able to put yourself in the other person's place and understand why they act the way they do even if you don't agree with it.

Visual Representation

Point of view

Contemporary or Personal Application

My mom was late to pick me up from school two days in a row, and I was really frustrated with her. I decided to consider her point of view. She is a single mom with a really stressful job that sometimes keeps her late. It doesn't mean she is blowing me off, but rather it was just something that happened that was out of her control. Furthermore, she was trying to be a responsible employee and complete her duties for the day so she could provide for our family.

ACTIVITY 11

Perspective-Based Review

DESCRIPTION Students create their own content reviews for each other and present them to the class based on perspectives other than their own. This activity provides students with options that develop higher-order thinking skills by integrating academic vocabulary as they read, write, and present content from a unique perspective.

Be another person or object and...

- Create an imaginary online profile (e.g., President Ronald Reagan's FB comments or Twitter page).

- Create a text or email conversation between two or more characters (e.g., Charlie Brown, Lucy, and Linus have a group text).

- Draw comic strips (e.g., a mixed number and an improper fraction go to lunch together).

- Tell me about yourself (e.g., use the Chatterpix app to take a picture, create the mouth, and talk for someone or something).

- Write letters between two friends (see example below as the sun writing to the moon after a lunar eclipse).

- Create a perspective-based quiz (e.g., Kahoot from a nucleus' perspective).

Students should be reminded of the following guidelines:
- They must use specific vocabulary from section
- The work must demonstrate specific ideas from the section
- They must be ready to explain the vocabulary to the class

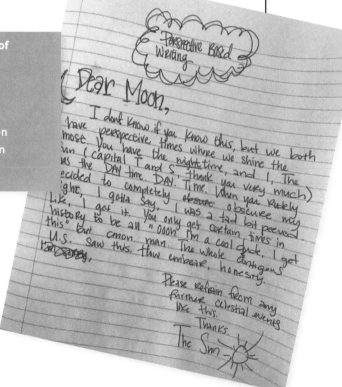

Vocabulary Storytelling (Group Dictado)

DESCRIPTION Students connect academic vocabulary (brick words) to create or retell a story by brainstorming with one another. Each student writes down the text that is developed as a group. During the writing phase, students verify grammar, spelling, and sentence structure with one another. The genre could be narrative, informational, or even a play script. Each academic vocabulary word must be used at least one time. Students then present their text orally to the class or through technology. Provide sentence stems as necessary to help get students started.

Alternatively, the teacher can show a short video and pause at predetermined points to have students illustrate so they can later retell the information using their own drawings.

DIRECTIONS

1. Review the vocabulary that each group will use. Aim for five to ten words that have already been presented and discussed.

2. Have students write down a word bank on the top of their journal pages.

3. Allow students to form three- to five-person teams.

4. Teams collaborate to create a script. This can be accomplished two ways: Students may wish to brainstorm first or choose one person to create the first sentence while everyone copies it down into his/her own journal.

5. As words are used, students check off words in their word banks. This ensures each word is used and spelled correctly.

EXAMPLES

A beginning ELL in middle school illustrates the Trojan Horse story as the teacher pauses at strategic points during a video recounting the tale. The student later retells the story using simple sentences and his drawings.

Content and language objectives are predetermined expectations that guide lessons and help students focus on specific goals during the lesson. They explain what students will learn and how they will learn it, and they define what students will be able to do by the end of each lesson. Effective content and language objectives are both measurable and observable (Seidlitz, Base, Lara, & Smith, 2015). English language learners need to be presented with objectives that are written in student-friendly language and appropriate for their level of language proficiency. They should be clearly posted in the classroom in a place that is visible and consistent every day. Ask yourself these questions:

Are my objectives written in student-friendly, academic language?

Are my objectives posted and visible for all to see?

Do I introduce my objectives at the beginning of each lesson?

Do I close my lesson by going back to the objectives and asking my students if they met the objectives?

Content and language objectives that are clearly displayed and addressed help students focus on specific goals. Implementing language objectives can be a powerful first step in ensuring that English language learners have equal access to the curriculum even though they may not be fully proficient in the language. This is because the second-language acquisition process requires opportunities for the language learner to be exposed to, practice with, and be assessed on their language skills (Echevarria, Vogt, & Short, 2008).

Content objectives are derived from state curriculum standards, and they reflect the content that is expected to be covered in a course of study. Students need to see, hear, and discuss the objectives prior to a lesson and have a clear understanding of what is going to be discussed in class that day. Often, teachers launch into the lesson without having the students really discuss what they're going to be covering in class that day. It is a bit like going into a movie having never seen the trailer. You don't know what to expect, you don't know the context or even the genre. As a language learner, you need to have a clear picture of what you're getting into. It is easy to start off confused and stay confused. This is why beginning the class with a clear objective is so important. Here is an example of a content objective for a social studies class:

Students will identify various points of view concerning the decision to rebel against the British prior to the American Revolution by creating a Venn diagram.

Language objectives are the goals we set to help students develop language through the content. Many teachers use their state's English language proficiency standards to help shape their language objectives. Language objectives are often required because they promote the use of the four domains of language (listening, speaking, reading, and writing) every day in class. By choosing a language objective that helps students develop their English while learning the content we ensure that students are not only going to be receiving comprehensible input, but they are also going to be producing language as well. Practicing listening, speaking, reading, and writing will inevitably strengthen their language development and regardless of which domain is selected, all other domains can be integrated. The following is an example of a language objective:

Students will write a letter expressing why they do not wish to rebel against the British during the American Revolution.

★ Content Objective

I will <u>(verb+TEKS)</u> by/using <u>(academic task)</u>.
  /   /   /
WHO   WHAT   HOW

FOR EXAMPLE:
I can identify the water cycle by creating and labeling a diagram.

I can see a student creating a diagram. This makes the objective **OBSERVABLE.**

I can measure whether or not the student identified the parts of the diagram and labeled them correctly. This makes the objective **MEASURABLE.**

Language Objective ★

I will <u>(domain/ELPS)</u> by/using <u>(specific words, phrases, or stems)</u>.
  /   /   /
WHO   WHAT   HOW

FOR EXAMPLE:
I can discuss with my partner the difference between _____ (condensation, precipitation, evaporation, etc.) and _____ (condensation, precipitation, evaporation, etc.) using:

_____ is the same as...

_____ and _____ have...

___ is similar/different than _____ in that...

I can see the students talking to one another. This makes the objective **OBSERVABLE.**

I can hear the students using specific words and phrases so they can develop academic language. This makes the objective **MEASURABLE.**

> >>> >>> When students hear terms and concepts out loud, they are more likely to recognize key words when they are used in the content throughout the lesson.

Reading the objectives aloud every day motivates students in several ways. Listening to, reading, and speaking the day's academic vocabulary that is embedded in the objective primes students for a greater understanding of the terms during the lesson. Reading the objectives before the learning occurs also allows students an opportunity to introduce themselves to what's going to be covered in class that day in the same way that a movie trailer prepares an audience for the film itself. Additionally, when students hear terms and concepts out loud, they are more likely to recognize key words when they are used in the content throughout the lesson.

There are many ways to motivate students to participate in the oral reading of the objective every day. The teacher can have the

students engage in choral reading (students read all together as a class) or use gestures or visuals that link the objective to experiences and ideas students are familiar with from past lessons, thus incorporating prior knowledge. A meaningful image paired with the objective can be a successful springboard for discussion. To get students to read loudly and with enthusiasm, the teacher can make the reading of the objectives game-like. For example, students can be divided across the classroom left and right, or girls can read first and then the boys. Students can stand up as they read the objectives, connecting physical movement (or "standing at attention") to the most important idea for the lesson. Native, or advanced, English speakers might be asked to repeat or rephrase the objectives in their own words. Bilingual students can translate orally or in writing to solidify the main ideas. Students can turn and talk to one another to summarize the objectives with sentence stems such as, "I think this means we're going to…" or "Today in class we're going to…" In doing this, students rephrase and personalize their understanding of the objectives based on what they see on the board.

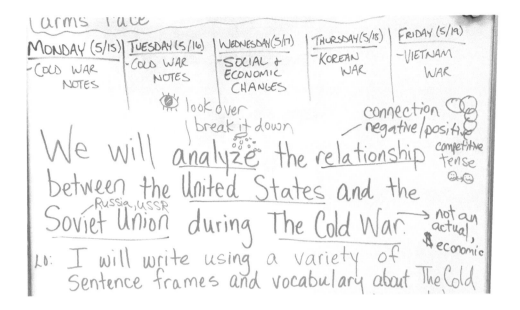

arms race

MONDAY (5/15)	TUESDAY (5/16)	WEDNESDAY(5/17)	THURSDAY(5/18)	FRIDAY (5/19)
-COLD WAR NOTES	-COLD WAR NOTES	-SOCIAL + ECONOMIC CHANGES	-KOREAN WAR	-VIETNAM WAR

look over / break it down

connection - negative/positive

competitive tense

We will <u>analyze</u> the <u>relationship</u> between the <u>United States</u> and the Soviet Union during The Cold War. _Russia, USSR_

→ not an actual, $ economic

LO: I will write using a variety of sentence frames and vocabulary about The Cold

The activities in this section are designed to pique students' interest and help them enjoy the possibilities of the day's lessons. For example, they may engage in a two-minute quick write about what they think they are going to learn about and then compare their ideas with another student. They glean ideas, understanding, and vocabulary from classmates, and it provides a hook into the lesson that will keep them engaged. Providing a meaningful hook alongside the objectives gives the students a way into the lesson that they might not otherwise have.

IDEAS FOR SHARING OBJECTIVES

- Use gestures or visuals that link the objective to student experiences
- Have students read loudly and with enthusiasm
- Make reading the objectives game-like
- Have students use physical movement when reading the objectives aloud
- Have students summarize objectives in their own language (English or home language)
- Have students rephrase and personalize the objectives

Quick Write, Compare, Revise

DESCRIPTION Students are given a short period of time (two to five minutes) to write as much as they possibly can about a topic. They are given time to share with a partner and to integrate ideas from their partner's writing into their own.

DIRECTIONS

Present students with a topic and several sentence stems to get them started in their writing. You might also want to use a meaningful visual to launch their writing.
Ask students to respect the writing time as a quiet, productive few minutes. Consider playing calm, non-lyrical writing music to set the mood.

It can be very motivating for students to see the teacher as a fellow writer; choose to either sit down and write next to a student who needs the most encouragement or roam around the room as you write in your journal in order to actively monitor student progress.

Students reread their own writing before sharing to help them prepare for reading aloud. As they share their writing with partners, each student pays close attention to differences between their writing and their partner's. After both partners share, they sit down and add an idea to their own writing that their partner mentioned. Sentence stems can help stimulate the conversation.

- It's interesting that you wrote about...
- I notice you mentioned...
- I am going to add...
- Your writing included...
- Can you please repeat the sentence about...?
- The idea I would like to add to my writing is...

Interactive Lecture

DESCRIPTION The lecture becomes interactive and more meaningful when the teacher strategically plans for structured conversation every five to ten minutes so that students can process what they are learning and make connections to background knowledge and personal experiences. With older or more advanced students, asking a compelling or unexpected question can motivate students to engage in the activity. Teachers may also propose a dilemma to students to engage them in a divergent discussion.

DIRECTIONS

1. With a copy of the lecture notes in hand, use a pen to insert sentence stems or questions you will pose to students for discussion.

2. Plan on pausing every five to ten minutes during the lecture. Consider where to pause based on your estimation of student engagement. For example, pausing after a short, powerful video clip or visual will often produce the liveliest conversations.

EXAMPLE

THE VIETNAM WAR: NOTES

1) The Vietnam War years were _1959 - 1975_ .
2) The U.S. sends soldiers _IN 1965_ .

Background

3) Vietnam was _COLONIZED_ by the French in 1874 and invaded by _JAPAN_ in 1945.
4) After _WW II_, North Vietnam fell under _COMMUNIST_ control and a _CIVIL WAR_ began against the south.
5) In _1955_, the U.S. began supporting South Vietnam with _TRAINING_ and _EQUIPMENT_ .
6) _HO CHI MINH_ became President of North Vietnam. _HANOI_ ~~SAIGON~~ became the capital.
7) _SAIGON_ became the capital of South Vietnam.
8) The Demarcation Line was near the _17th PARALLEL_ .

The Domino Theory

9) If one Southeast Asia country falls to _COMMUNISM_ the others will _FALL_ .
10) The U.S. response is ... _CONTAINMENT_ .

Ask students: What other countries have experienced Civil Wars? What caused these wars?

The cause of the civil war in _____ was _____.

Ask students: What root word do you see in the word containment and what does it mean to you?

The root word of containment is _____. It means _____.

Start with a Spark: Annotating the Objective

DESCRIPTION Imagine for a moment that you walk into a restaurant for the first time. There are no menus on the table or the wall, and a minute after you enter you are asked to order. Huh? You have no idea what is even being offered! This is how students (particularly ELLs) feel when they enter a classroom and are expected to understand what is happening (and why) without any clear goal being discussed. Spending a few minutes at the beginning of class orally discussing the learning objective and highlighting key vocabulary is like going into a restaurant with a solid menu displayed on the wall and a knowledgeable greeter or server there to explain your choices. It may take five to ten minutes the first time, but after a few classes students know what to expect and it will only take two to three minutes. The time invested in presenting the objectives clearly will eliminate confusion and save a significant amount of time that might otherwise be spent reiterating the purpose of the day's learning.

DIRECTIONS

1. Introduce the restaurant metaphor, taking time to ensure that all students are sharing their experiences. It is absolutely vital that students understand and accept the importance of analyzing the objective because this process will be done on a daily basis.

2. Read the objectives aloud, with the goal of eventually having a student read them.

3. Utilize a randomizing technique to select a student to list any key words or words they do not understand.

4. Underline these words and work through them one by one, asking for students to rephrase or define key words. Add these words, phrases, and definitions to the side as well as some quick visuals. Do this for both the content and language objectives.

5. Have students turn and tell a partner what the goal of the lesson (a.k.a. the menu) for today is in their own words.

6. Invite one or two students to share what they or their partner said.

7. Don't forget to review and assess understanding in the middle or at the end of the lesson. See how many times you can have students verbalize the key words throughout the lesson (via QSSSA/structured conversations) and use them in writing.

EXAMPLES

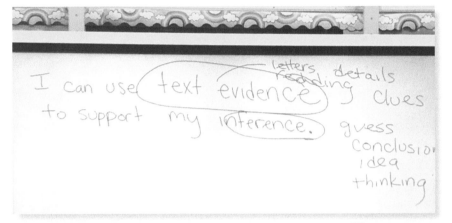

Elementary

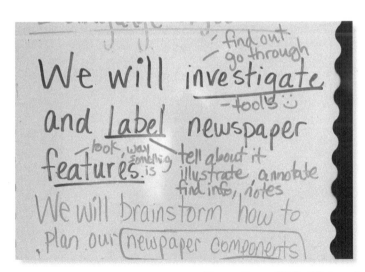

Secondary (U.S. History)

B ⟫ MEETING CONTENT AND LANGUAGE GOALS

Flip Cards

DESCRIPTION This card activity encourages students to interact with key vocabulary as they engage in meaningful conversations with peers.

DIRECTIONS

1. Have students write down key vocabulary words on index cards, one word per card. (Cards can be prepared in advance, if necessary.)

2. In pairs or small groups, have students place the cards on their desks with the words facing up.

3. As students read through a text, practice word problems, or engage in structured conversations, they flip the cards over as they identify or use them. Once they have flipped over all the cards, they earn a check. Then they start over. The element of friendly competition can be introduced by tracking which team uses all of their words first.

MEANINGFUL ENDEAVORS

One way to welcome English language learners into the classroom community is to invite them to be a part of something bigger than themselves. As they participate in meaningful projects or activities that go beyond the classroom walls, students will experience a greater sense of belonging and acceptance. Teachers can provide meaningful endeavors to give ELLs purpose for their activities, then use those activities as vehicles to drive content concepts and specific objectives. For example, a school garden is a great opportunity for learning in all content areas. In places where that is not feasible, student projects like sending books to schools in an impoverished country or fundraising for a needy population in their community can also foster feelings of acceptance and belonging. Many students also enjoy Skyping with a class across the country and writing letters to penpals in another city. Students might create a classroom book that can be published and incorporated into their school library or distributed in their community. They could also participate in developing a community project such as going to visit different places like nursing homes or preschools to share their reading, songs, and writing in a meaningful format.

Meaningful endeavors are a type of project-based learning, and they integrate easily into the Language Experience Approach (Krajcik & Blumenfeld, 2006; Nessel & Dixon, 2008). The Language Experience Approach is successful because students have an opportunity to

English language learners measure and graph plant growth; a student-led composting project uses leftover food from the cafeteria

connect through shared experiences (see pg. 65). Meaningful endeavors take cooperative learning beyond the classroom walls. Students whose teachers implement cooperative learning strategies inside and outside the classroom learn to communicate positively with peers and master more academic material than students whose teachers require that they work mostly in isolation (Calderon, 1989). Students also exhibit higher self-esteem, and learning motivation increases dramatically. English language learners in particular benefit from group experiences and activities that require them to listen, speak, read, and write with peers.

Because English language learners come from different backgrounds, they don't often feel a sense of being part of a community within their classrooms immediately upon entering school. Meaningful endeavors are a way to engage them in the community of learners in the classroom, and let ELLs know that they are part of a group of people that is making a difference.

Meaningful endeavors inspire an authentic desire to communicate. When teachers apply meaningful endeavors as a vehicle for learning content, students are not only given the opportunities to produce language, but they are given a reason to do so. For example, they want to communicate with a pen pal who lives in another state or even in a different country. They want to communicate with an elderly person at a nursing home, who needs a visit or who is knowledgeable about something they are interested in. They want to be able to show off their products at a school business fair. If they are selling small plants they have grown from seeds, they want to be able to communicate what they have done and why it is important to them.

Many ELLs associate English exclusively with school because their native language is used in the home and community. For these children, it can be difficult to see exactly how increasing their proficiency is going to help them in real life when it has not been needed thus far outside the school walls. If we can make that link between what they are learning in class and what they can do with it going forward, we're bridging their two worlds.

Margaret Rutaquio is an inspiring teacher who guided a classroom of English language learners to participate in community service projects. Students wrote about their meaningful endeavors on a blog.

>>> >>> Our English language learners' sparks, diligence, and perseverance toward graduation and success are the main goals of the ELL Leadership Class. In this class our ELLs are encouraged to hone their communication and leadership skills, interact and collaborate with peers, and celebrate the attribute of kindness with humanity's beauty through highlighting student community service.

The ELL Leadership Class of South Garland HS (2015-2016) was composed of English language learners with proficiency levels ranging from Beginner to Advanced High. In addition, students were from different grade levels, SES, and languages. Despite the range of differences, the classes were united in one commitment—service leadership. Thus, in that school year alone, the classes ended the year with a total of 33 community service projects.

Margaret Rutaquio, ELL Leadership Teacher

Ms. Rutaquio's Story ★

One community service project that was close to my heart was our book drive to the Philippines. Coming from a third-world country and growing up loving reading but not having enough books, reading became one of my advocacies. The students of the ELL Leadership Class were able to get donations to fill up boxes full of books for elementary students. Since language learning was an embedded part of the class, the students were required to write about each project or activity that they participated in. For this particular service project, the students wrote letters of hope for the elementary students in the Philippines and inserted them inside the books that they had sent.

Most of the students wrote more than one letter since the students were excited about the fact that their letters would reach kids who lived in another part of the world. The students searched for quotes of hope and shared some of their own experiences in the letters. Some beginner students wrote using a combination of English and Spanish so they could express themselves better. After the activity, the students were asked to write about their process as well as their reflections in their blogs, which are called "Good Deeds Blogs."

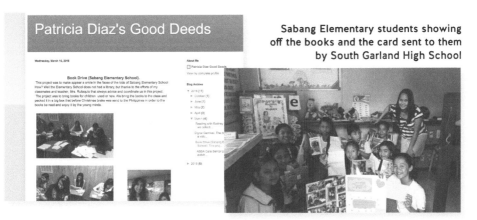

Sabang Elementary students showing off the books and the card sent to them by South Garland High School

A year after this service project, Patricia Diaz, whose blog post is shown above, spoke in front of more than 200 ELL students during our sixth annual Youth Summit. In her speech, she spoke about how important this project was to her heart because when she was in El Salvador she was not allowed to check out books, since only older kids could use them. Thus, she worked very hard on this project, as she remembered having experienced the longing to read without resources available.

Meaningful endeavors can be accomplished in any content area. Take math, for example. Something as simple as calculating figures when establishing and running a school store, identifying geometric shapes on the playground, or designing an appropriate playscape for younger students can be very meaningful in math classrooms. When students are aware of the real-life application of the content, the value of the lesson increases beyond the limited incentive of successful academic performance.

I first experienced the magic of cross-curricular learning when I started a school garden at the elementary school in Boerne, Texas, where I was teaching. Students enjoyed applying math concepts, creating stories and poetry, and learning about history, all while spending time in the great outdoors. The unit culminated in the harvesting of the fruits (and vegetables and herbs) of their labor.

Finding ways to provide meaningful endeavors was challenging for me because it required me to think a little bit outside of the box. It meant going beyond the effort required to generate my typical lesson plan. It required putting in a little forethought as to how to carry out the project, and looking for support from teachers— even from other schools and cities—who had done similar projects and could offer guidance. It may be challenging for educators to find the right resources to be able to successfully negotiate these projects with students. The outcome, however, is so powerful that it is worth the effort.

Language Experience Approach

DESCRIPTION In a Language Experience Approach (LEA), students use their own vocabulary, language patterns, and shared experiences to create texts for reading and to make the reading process meaningful and enjoyable (Boyle & Peregoy, 2012).

When preparing the classroom to take part in LEA, it is important to encourage the students to communicate as naturally as possible, and to choose a topic that is relevant and engaging to all students as a shared classroom experience (Nessel & Dixon, 2008). LEA motivates ELLs because they get to discuss shared experiences with their classmates in a low-stress environment.

DIRECTIONS

1. Discuss a shared and/or familiar experience, such as a field trip, classroom project, or common activity.

2. Record and reframe student statements on chart paper as they discuss the shared experience in their own words. At this point, students are connecting oral to written language by seeing their own thoughts and words recorded on paper.

3. Once constructed, read the text out loud to the students, modeling the sounds of the language with expression. Have students practice reading the text several times, with assistance if needed.

4. Guide the students in recognizing specific words, and help promote the development of decoding skills such as context, phonics, and structures of the language.

5. Have the students use the shared text as a springboard for writing original compositions.

6. Consider preserving copies of LEA stories to be available for self/selected reading material. Students often enjoy revisiting their shared stories.

EXAMPLE

Elementary:

Dissect a pumpkin in the fall. (Tip: Pumpkin patches will often donate to teachers after Halloween.) Have students estimate the number of seeds found in two different pumpkins. Rinse and toast the seeds to enjoy as a class. Have students add different spices to small bags of pumpkins and sample. Follow steps two through five for math reasoning, taste sensations poetry, or procedural writing.

Secondary:

Students consider two to three locations on campus for a small school garden or beautification project. Walk the grounds with students to get a visual, and take notes and drawings on pros/cons for each location and idea. Students then form small groups based on their preferred options. Follow steps two through five for developing persuasive writing as a class and then individually or in small groups.

Classroom Book

DESCRIPTION Students work together to create a classroom book that can become part of the classroom (and school) library.

DIRECTIONS

1. Present a main idea for students to explore. This could be thematic (our school garden, things to do in our city or neighborhood, family, food, etc.) or directly tied to content (geometry in our world, historical figures, body systems, etc.).

2. Have each student journey through the writing process to complete a page or two with text as well as illustrations or photographs.

3. Have the students revisit the published book as a class or on their own. This will give students pride and a sense of ownership for their literary accomplishment.

Note: There are many websites that can also publish the book with a hard cover, so families can have the option to purchase a copy for their homes. You can also bind it yourself with a comb binding for a nominal fee at a copy store (unless you're lucky enough to have comb binder at your school).

EXAMPLES

Cultivating
RELATIONSHIPS

Who motivates someone to learn in school? More often than not, it's teachers. As teachers, our personalities and temperaments, as well as the way in which we form relationships with students are significant factors in motivating learners.

A student's interest in a subject can be virtually ruined by an unenjoyable educator, while a previously uninteresting subject can become incredibly engaging with an enthusiastic teacher whose passion for the topic is infectious. Similarly, the students' ability to understand and build rapport with fellow classmates has a great effect on their willingness to participate and communicate with their peers in class.

My own journey toward bilingualism was deeply affected by a teacher. After having a miserable first exposure to Spanish (the teacher was fired the year I took the class), I walked into my second year with very low expectations. Much to my surprise, this enthusiastic teacher got to know each student and had us singing and dancing to Shakira in no time. She even wrote a caring note at the end of the year to encourage me to continue learning Spanish. That note holds a prominent place in my high school scrapbook today.

A note from my high school Spanish teacher in 1997.

My high school principal made it a point to handwrite a note for each student before they graduated.

Querida Lora Beth,   24 mayo

Yo te deseo mucha suerte en tu vida y un futuro muy brillante.

Eres una persona muy talentosa e inteligente. Fue un placer enseñarte el año pasado. Favor de continuar el estudio de español.

Felicidades en tu graduación

Sinceramente,
Sra. Webb

Dear Lora Beth:

Words can not express how much we appreciate everything you have done for B.HS. You made a positive difference every single day you were at school. For these reasons and countless others, I am proud and honored to present you with this scholarship in my name. STUART cavender the owner of cavender chevrolet/ olds/ Geo provided the money. Good bless!

Sincerely,
Mr. C.

'Everybody is Somebody at Boerne High School'

Teachers who invest time and energy getting to know about their students' lives beyond the classroom are able to build stronger relationships that will serve as the foundation for the whole year in the classroom. These relationships also help teachers make connections between content-area knowledge and students' personal lives, thereby making the content applicable and interesting.

Many times ELL newcomers come into a school, and they're not familiar with the environment or the culture of the personnel at school. This can even be true for students and teachers who speak the same language. For example, you might have a teacher from Mexico and students from El Salvador. The teacher can bridge the cultural (and even linguistic) divide by putting forth the effort to get to know students.

Beginning the process of connecting with students from less familiar cultural backgrounds can be daunting. After all, we are not all experts in world cultures and geography. But what seems like a deficit is actually a wonderful opportunity for the student to become the teacher. Admitting a lack of knowledge and expressing a desire to learn is a powerful way for us as teachers to practice what we preach.

Sometimes we have misconceptions about our students' cultures. Media often exposes us to negative perceptions or overgeneralizations of certain cultural groups, whether or not they are grounded in actual fact. When we make the effort to get to know our students as individuals, as opposed to believing generalizations about cultural groups, we open ourselves up to forming authentic and positive relationships.

One simple thing we can do to overcome such misunderstandings is to learn about our students' families. Ask students to bring in pictures, artifacts that represent their home life, or simple items like clothing that represents their culture. We can also express curiosity about the languages represented in the class and learn a few words or phrases. This effort can make a significant difference as to how our students respond to us, as they will recognize that we are reaching out and connecting.

Displaying a few words in a student's native language shows you care and helps foster relationships among classmates.

We must not only make an effort to cultivate relationships with our newcomers, we must also cultivate relationships with our long-term ELLs. The first step in this process is to identify the students as a group needing additional support. Teachers and administrators need to know these students by name and know the data related to their academic performance. Interestingly, current research regarding best practices for meeting the needs of these students focuses on the importance of cultivating relationships (Olsen, 2014).

Relationships play a significant role in whether the affective filter will be high or low. Just as in our social relationships, we feel comfortable speaking to someone who knows us as an individual and can relate to us in some way. As teachers, when we get to know our students in a deeper way we are more likely to feel comfortable engaging those students in class. When we become more aware of students who are not participating or who may feel excluded from the class conversation, we can reach out to them to establish a positive relationship. We can get to know our students by asking questions to explore their interests and talents as well as their family background and home environments.

CLASSROOM ROUTINES

While all students benefit from predictable classroom routines, the difference they can make for ELLs is particularly noteworthy. Regular habits, actions, and activities that are part of the daily classroom procedures allow ELLs to know what to expect in a classroom. For example, when a student enters a well-ordered classroom, she knows, "This is what is going to happen every day: I'm going to be greeted by my teacher at the door, I'm going to find my seat and put my materials away, I will recite The Pledge of Allegiance, then I will complete a warm-up activity and preview the objective."

When English language learners come into a familiar environment in which they know what to expect, they feel more comfortable and are more willing to participate. The confidence this inspires sets a positive tone for the classroom and lowers the affective filter because the likelihood of the student experiencing surprise, shock, or frustration is minimized.

Classroom routines are also important when students are listening, speaking, reading, and writing. Language development accelerates when students know the structures for the linguistic exchanges that are prominent during those classroom routines. For example, if they know that they're going to stand up and say the Pledge of Allegiance every morning, they can work on memorizing the Pledge

Honor the Texas Flag; I pledge allegiance to thee, Texas, one state under God, one and indivisible.

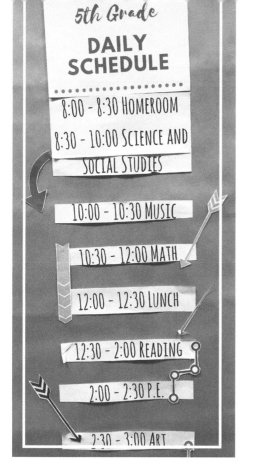

managing disciplinary issues that we may end up applauding (or worse, ignoring) quiet students, often unaware that these quiet students, who may be ELLs, are paying a high price with their silence. Students who sit silently day after day do not have the opportunity to develop language or content knowledge.

Establishing classroom routines does not mean scripting each moment of each day, without leaving room for surprises, spontaneity, or "teachable moments." There is definitely a place for both routine and spontaneity; they are not mutually exclusive. As teachers, we often thrive on creativity, and we do not want to stifle our inventiveness. A few routines at the beginning of class can be very short and concise, possibly taking five minutes or less to complete. The remainder of class time can be more flexible within the parameters of the general agenda. The main goal of consistent classroom routines is to establish and maintain a sense of community.

of Allegiance and feel confident enough to participate fully in that experience every day. Likewise, if the teacher generally starts with a warm-up, they know where to find the warm-up in the classroom. Students will look for it on the screen or perhaps on a small piece of paper located in the same place each day as they walk in. Students also have a sense of how much time is going to be taken up with each routine and what verbalization is expected from them during those routines. If the teacher sets up a routine in which students regularly compare their work after a warm-up, English language learners will know that every day they're going to get to talk to someone next to them and work through the warm-up together.

Students who challenge us with inappropriate or disruptive behavior can overshadow students who are quiet and compliant. So much energy can be exerted

AFFIRMATIONS

A great routine to establish for English language learners, and indeed all students, is to choose a short set of enjoyable, smile-provoking affirmations that are known by the entire class.

Affirmations are simple choral responses usually accompanied by a gesture that tells students they did something well. We can use affirmations after activities such as structured conversations or presentations, when a student takes a risk to share, or when the class simply follows directions efficiently.

These are some examples:

· Clapping in a circle for a "round of applause"

· Three snaps and a clap

· Pretending to strum a guitar while saying, "Thank you, thank you very much" in your best Elvis Presley voice

· Pretending to throw a lasso while shouting, "Yee-haw!"

Opening Ceremonies

DESCRIPTION Create a regular routine for starting the class or day that honors various languages and cultures.

DIRECTIONS

1. Learn the proper greetings in the various languages your students speak.

2. Have a poster with various greetings.

3. Greet students at door using different native languages spoken by ELLs in your class.

4. As your students enter, interact with them in ways that honor their presence (handshake, high five, fist bump, elbow bump, or silly face).

5. Explain to the students how to pronounce a particular greeting from the chart.

6. Establish a specific daily procedure for beginning the class by reading the objectives (i.e., student volunteer, teacher reads then pauses, etc.).

SAMPLE DIALOGUE

Today our greeting comes from the country of ____. This is where it is found on the map. (Point to the country on the map.)

The greeting is pronounced_____. Let's all try it together.

Snap-up Wrap-up

DESCRIPTION This activity closes a lesson and offers a chance for ELLs to consider what they will take away and what progress they made toward the learning goal or objective. It can also be used as formative assessment by the teacher to determine student readiness to continue or the need for clarification and/or additional instruction.

DIRECTIONS

1. Have an official time set aside at the end of class to wrap up the lesson and help yourself and the students reflect on learning.

2. Include an oral or written response from students as part of the conclusion. You can also use a response signal like the one in the illustration. If students hold their fist at chest level as they indicate their leveled response, you can see them, and their responses are less revealing to their peers.

3. Use oral or written responses from students as assessments or to help guide future instruction.

STUDENT INTERESTS

Discovering student interests can be a great way to tap into what motivates students internally, and it doesn't have to take a lot of time on the teacher's part. We can pose a simple question and ask students to share what they're good at, what they enjoy doing, or something about themselves that other people might not know. We can ask students to share one thing about their parents, one thing about their siblings, one thing about their home, or one thing about their native country. These are very simple ways in which we can get to know our students. It is particularly important that we tap into the interests of our English language learners, as they might not know how much we (and the other students) are interested in their individual stories and lives.

Likewise, students enjoy knowing their teacher as a person and not just as their educator. Students benefit from observing that their teachers have a personal interest in the content as well.

Sharing our struggles as well as our successes and talents can cultivate positive relationships with our students. My first year teaching, I lost my beloved dog. It happened right before school one day; he somehow got out of the yard and got hit by a car. I was devastated. I even wore his little dog tag to school on my necklace. I cried in front of my students, and their response was overwhelming. They were so compassionate and interested in what my dog was like and how I felt. I didn't know if I should hide my feelings and try to carry on with class as usual or if I should let my true emotions show. By allowing myself to be vulnerable and cry in front of them, I actually got to know my students better that day. Quite a few students had lost pets or had left pets in their home countries when they came to the United States. This sharing of interests actually became a vehicle for getting to know my students and strengthening the sense of community in our classroom.

When trying to engage students' interests, we must resist making ungrounded assumptions based on our limited knowledge of their home country. We all have our own mental list of generalizations we have heard, but our popular culture knowledge of a certain group may or may not be applicable to the students in our classroom. I once asked a group of students from various countries in Central America who a famous male would be, expecting them to name a soccer star or pop icon. Instead, they named El Chapo, a well-known drug cartel leader who had recently been in the media. We used that as an example of a (in)famous person as it related to an article they were about to read. Opening up conversations rather than making assumptions is an effective way of tapping into students' interests and backgrounds.

Even though students come from distinct backgrounds, they all have shared school experiences whether they have been in school together a day, a week, or years. I began using Schoologues (see pg. 82) once

>>> >>> Opening up conversations rather than making assumptions is an effective way of tapping into students' interests and backgrounds.

I realized the power of connecting through these shared experiences. Students have common experiences with recess, the lunch room, and before- and after-school routines like taking the bus or walking. They have experiences with after-school activities or specials classes like PE, music, that can serve a source material. Asking students "What are you doing in art?" or "What interests you about that?" and then tying that information to other content helps cement their learning. For example, if I discovered that my students were enjoying papier-mâché in art class, I could bring that into my lesson and connect that with World History, or use it as a basis to choose texts for reading. I might have students recreate ancient monuments out of papier-mâché, or have them read an article on its use in ancient Egypt. Students who participate in team sports and clubs (band, drama, cheer, etc.) will perk up when you mention how their interests relate to the content. You may even help ELLs discover a new

interest when you and their classmates mention and describe these possible extracurricular activities, as they might be unaware of what is available at school and in the community.

Mini-Conference Logs

DESCRIPTION This idea came from conducting writing conferences with my fourth grade students. At the time, we were required to keep anecdotal notes on each student as we conferenced with them about their writing. I started noticing how it not only helped improve writing, but it also enriched the relationship we had. Each session was like a little meeting of the minds, and we all looked forward to these few one-on-one moments. As they read their stories out loud, I got to know them as individuals. I wrote down little details I learned about their experiences, friends, families, pets, and their likes and dislikes. One day when I was working with middle school students, it dawned on me how helpful this could be for all classrooms. There are almost always times in class when students are working individually or in small groups on a task, so why not capitalize on this time to get to know students as I encourage them academically? For teachers of ELLs, this time also provides an education about students' home countries, native languages, and cultural customs.

DIRECTIONS

1. Create a spreadsheet based on the example on the next page for each class of students.

2. Print them out and place them in a conference journal (a three-ring binder or composition notebook).

3. As you meet with each student, consider asking two to three meaningful questions.

4. See how much you can get them to share about themselves and the academic task they are working on.

5. Try to limit each session to three to five minutes, but don't be too strict. If you are engaged in a meaningful conversation, bring it to a close gently as opposed to abruptly.

6. After you finish your conference, note the date you met with the student in the spreadsheet, and include a few notes as to the nature of the conversation.

7. Use the record of your conversations to create a resource of information when you meet again. These notes may also come in handy when you meet with parents.

QUESTION IDEAS
- What are you working on?
- How's it going?
- How can I support you?
- How does this relate to your life?
- What areas of strength do you notice?
- What areas for growth?
- What is your goal for our next meeting?

Class: ENGLISH 8   Section: 04W   Period:4

STUDENT	M	Tu	W	Th	F	M	Tu	W	Th	F
Andrerson, Oliver M.										
Colina, Becca J.										
Hildebrandt, Ben G.										
Fillmore, Anna C.										
Nunez, Chloe M.										
Patton, Ava D.										
Perez, Christopher D.										
Rodriquez, Matthew D.										
Suarez, Aaron W.										
Toure, Ahmed M.										
Vasquez, Emily O.										
Zavala, Domingo A.										

Dom –
3/1 testing – key terms in the Q- able to tell me
text evidence (write # of scene & line
next to the Q)
eliminating wrong choices
sweet kid (parents from Coahuila, MX)

3/1 Hussein – Thesaurus – (testing)
Dictionary – Ironic – use Text Evidence
The importance of understanding the vocab
(Ex: ironic, honest) from test question
(from Iraq) Gave personal example of
parents from Iraq and don't speak
Arabic (irony)

Pick a Pic

DESCRIPTION Using pictures that are meaningful to them (either on their phone, as a print out, or in a book or card) students communicate information about their pictures to their peers using academic language. This activity promotes both social and academic interaction and helps students share important personal interests. It also has the added benefit of increasing students' oral fluency and elaboration skills. Later, as you transition students to talking about content-based visuals, they are able to generate and verbalize more ideas.

DIRECTIONS

1. Present a picture from your own life to your students. They will enjoy getting to know more about you.

2. Model how to use sentence stems to describe or explain the photo. Consider using academic words and and phrases that include targeted vocabulary terms or previously taught phrases and words.

3. As a model, engage in a structured conversation with another student.

4. Have students share with each other. Randomize who shares with the whole class.

5. As students become more comfortable sharing about their lives in academic language, transition to using content-based visuals such as illustrations from books.

We pulled our phone pic. We choose the last 5th pic from our phone and the sentence stem share →

SENTENCE STEM EXAMPLES

This picture indicates how I _____.

Based on the information found in this picture, you could infer that _____.

The ____ depicted in this picture is _____.

The best description of ____ is ____.

EXTENSION

This activity can easily be adapted by using realia from your lesson, or meaningful visuals from a content concept you are teaching. For example, in a science lesson students can choose from a variety of rocks with various physical properties to use in their structured conversations.

Life Links

DESCRIPTION Students consider commonalities and differences between themselves and people they learn about through history and literacy. They share ideas about characters and personal connections in order to gain a deeper understanding of the content. Students can draw connections between themselves and a character or figure in history, between two others, between events, and between texts.

DIRECTIONS

1. Identify key individuals from text or key concepts from a section.

2. Model how to use sentence stems that connect the individuals or concepts to a student's personal life.

I am similar to ___ in that ___.

I am different to ____ in that ___.

I would like to speak to ____ because...

If I could invite someone from ____ over for dinner,
I would invite ____ because...

_____ reminds me of something in my family because...

I would like to be similar to ____ because...

A challenge I faced similar to _____ was...

I can imagine why ____ decided to ___, because...

Given the situation that ____ was in, _____.

If I found myself in a situation like _____'s, I might _____.

3. Have students share their responses with each other and discuss commonalities and differences.

Schoologues

DESCRIPTION When we talk about accessing prior knowledge for English language learners, part of the reason why it's so significant is that it enables us to find input that will not just be comprehensible but also compelling. We don't know what's going to be interesting or engaging for students until we get to know them and access their background knowledge. Krashen & Bland talk about compelling input (2014). Input doesn't just need to be comprehensible to kids, it also needs to be compelling. In fact, it may need to be compelling in order to be comprehensible. Compelling input means input (such as printed material or things students are going to hear) that intrigues them so that they will chase after it. The material is so naturally engaging that their minds are craving more after the experience.

SCHOOLOGUES TO CONSIDER
- school clubs, teams, mascots
- campus features (outdoor areas, cafeteria, track, school grounds, stores within walking distance)
- elective classes (art, music, band, athletics, computer class, etc.)
- famous or well-known people associated with the school
- major achievements of the school in the past
- suggestions for improving instruction
- aspects of school climate that could be improved

OUR SCHOOLOGUES			
In our class	In other classes	Around campus	Near campus

CONNECT *with* COMMUNITY

There are experiences we may never share, but we can empathize with students. Even if we have not immigrated to another country, if we have not struggled to learn a second language, this does not mean we cannot connect with them and create a sense of community.

A significant part of cultivating relationships is exploring how English language learners and their families live within their communities. What activities do they participate in? Where do they live geographically? Do they live in apartments? In single or multi-family homes? On ranches? Who else lives in the community? Do their parents, grandparents, aunts, and uncles live nearby? Where do their parents work within the community? What businesses do their families own? Learning these things about our students helps us cultivate those relationships because we know the students' everyday experiences outside school.

Many times families move to the United States in search of opportunities or because of struggles they've had in their native countries: war, natural disaster, or terrorism. Some parents of ELLs may have been forced to give up their vocations when they left their home countries. If we investigate a little bit, we often discover that the students' parents might have been dentists, doctors, or business owners. Something that we can do as teachers is invite our students to share what their parents' talents are with questions like these:

What are some special skills your parents have?

What kinds of jobs have your family members had?

Asking these vital questions shows newcomer English language learners that you value what they have accomplished here in the United States, what they accomplished in their home countries, and who they are as individuals. Invite family members to be guest speakers in your classroom and share their stories to deepen your students' understanding of their classmates. By building relationships with both our ELLs and their families, we strengthen the bond between classroom and community, and highlight the influence that family members can have on a child's academic experience.

When we establish a positive relationship with parents, we can emphasize the significance of native-language literacy development and maybe even suggest activities for them to do in their homes, such as reading to their children and providing opportunities for the children to have books in their native language. It's important that students continue native language literacy practices because they correlate directly with their ability to transfer language skills into the new language (Escamilla, et al., 2009). Not only does native-language literacy help students maintain their identities as speakers of their native language, but it also allows for a continued relationship between their extended family that may not be learning English. There are many ways we can show we value students' native languages and cultures, especially in a multilingual classroom in which many languages are represented.

Game Day

DESCRIPTION This activity involves inviting friends and family members into the class to play academic-based games as a way of motivating students. They can show off skills they have acquired in class and, in turn, gain deeper understanding by explaining the games to others.

> **A FEW GAMES TO INCLUDE**
> - Math games
> - Literacy games with familiar books and characters
> - Bingo with academic vocabulary and pictures or descriptions
> - Partner reading station
> - "Read the room" with a parent

DIRECTIONS

1. Select which games you will play.
2. Ask students to translate invitations to parents into their native languages.
3. Send out the invitation to parents.
4. Review the games students will play with their families a day or two before.
5. Organize stations around the room with visuals that show how each game is played.
6. Consider providing light snacks or asking parents to bring refreshments.

Consider varying the times for these get togethers to accommodate the working schedules of students' parents.

Note: Phone calls can also be very helpful; if you have difficulty communicating with parents, you can have the student help you. Parents appreciate a positive phone call!

Progressive Potluck

DESCRIPTION Progressive Potluck is an inviting way to showcase the cultures each of your ELLs bring to the classroom. As students share with each other, they begin to value each classmate as a unique individual and a valuable asset to the class. An event like a casual potluck can also bring families together to meet and mingle as they share some food.

DIRECTIONS

1. Select a group of topics for discussion (try to print topics in students' native languages with visuals).

2. Arrange the room into stations, with discussion topics at each station.

3. Invite parents in, and have them bring one food item that is common in their native culture, a traditional dish, or something that's simply special to their family.

4. Have families travel with their children from table to table enjoying food samples and having discussions about set topics.

5. Play music from different cultures for guests to enjoy as families socialize.

TOPICS YOU MIGHT INCLUDE

• Family members

• World maps for locating home countries

• Realia that will be used in class

• Photos or visuals related to upcoming lessons

• Picture cards to match with vocabulary terms

Community Talent Tap

DESCRIPTION Explore the talent that your ELL families bring by asking students to interview a family member. Older students can conduct interviews for oral histories of community members. They can practice with each other in class first, using sentence stems. This practice involves all four domains of language and also provides a bank of possible guest speakers for future events, all while you discover how family members' talents, hobbies, and careers relate to content you cover in class.

a

DIRECTIONS

1. Ask students to explore the background of an important adult in their lives, such as a parent, guardian, neighbor, or role model from the community.

2. Provide students with a short survey of questions to ask. For best results, have students work together to draft the survey. Students may translate the survey into the language of their family member if necessary.

3. Provide sufficient time for students to conduct interviews on their own, and if necessary translate portions of the interview into English.

4. Have students highlight one or two specific details from the interview they would like to share with the class. Have them teach the class one to two words in their native language and explain their meanings through words or visuals.

Extension: Invite parents in to talk to students about their talents, hobbies, or careers. This is an excellent opportunity for students to practice speaking in English as they help translate for parents. Furthermore, students are usually fascinated by guest speakers!

Activity Index ★

Bibliography

Ada, A. F. (2003). *A magical encounter: Latino children's literature in the classroom.* Boston, MA: Allyn & Bacon/Longman Publishers.

Amato, P. A. (2010). *Making it happen: From interactive to participatory language teaching: Evolving theory and practice.* White Plains, NY: Pearson Education.

Asher, J. J. (1969). The total physical response approach to second language learning. *The Modern Language Journal, 53*(1), 3-17.

Ashton-Warner, S. (1986). *Teacher.* New York: Simon and Schuster.

Auerbach, E. (2000). Creating participatory learning communities: Paradoxes and possibilities. In J. K. Hall & W. G. Eggington (Eds.), *The sociopolitics of English language teaching* (pp. 143–164). Clevedon, England: Multilingual Matters.

Calderon, M. (1989). Cooperative learning for LEP students. *Intercultural Development Research Association Newsletter, 16*(9), 1-7.

Campano, G. (2007). *Immigrant students and literacy: Reading, writing, and remembering.* New York: Teachers College Press.

Cisneros, S. (2013). *The house on mango street.* Visala, CA: Vintage.

Curtis, C. P. (2013). *The Watsons go to Birmingham: 1963.* New York: Yearling.

Dewey, J. (1959). *Dewey on education.* New York: Columbia University.

Dixon, C. N., & Nessel, D. D. (1983). *Language experience approach to reading and writing: Language experience reading for second language learners.* Hayward, CA: Alemany Press.

Echevarria, J., Vogt, M., & Short, D. (2017). *Making content comprehensible for English learners: The SIOP Model (5th ed.).* New York: Pearson.

Escalante, L. B. (2012). "¡Luces, camara, accion!": A classroom teacher research analysis of dual language students translanguaging through one-act plays. (Doctoral Dissertation). San Antonio, TX: The University of Texas at San Antonio. Retrieved from: https://eric.ed.gov/?q=laughter&pg=7&id=ED549067

Escamilla, K., Geisler, D., Hopewell, S., Sparrow, W., & Butvilofsky, S. (2009). Using writing to make cross-language connections from Spanish to English. In C. Rodriguez (Ed.), *Achieving literacy success with English language learners,* 141-156. Reading, OH: Reading Recovery Council of North America.

Freire, P. (1998). *Pedagogy of freedom: Ethics, democracy, and civic courage.* Lanham, MD: Rowman & Littlefield.

Herrera, S. G., Perez, D. R., & Escamilla, K. (2015). *Teaching reading to English language learners: Differentiated literacies (2nd ed.).* Boston, MA: Pearson.

Huang, I. Y.(2008). Role play for ESL/EFL children in the English classroom. *The Internet TESL Journal, 14*(2). Retrieved from: http://iteslj.org/Techniques/Huang-RolePlay.html

Ibarra, H., & Seidlitz, J. (2016). *Sometimes.* Irving, TX: Canter Press.

Jiménez, F. (1999). *The circuit.* New York: Houghton Mifflin Harcourt.

Kagan, S., & Kagan, L. (1992). *Cooperative learning course workbook.* San Clemente, CA: Kagan Cooperative Learning.

Kohn, A. (1993). Choices for children: Why and how to let students decide. *Phi Delta Kappan, 75*(1), 8-16. Retrieved from: https://www.alfiekohn.org/article/choices-children

Krajcik, J. S., & Blumenfeld, P. C. (2006). Project-based learning. In R. K. Sawyer (Ed.), *The Cambridge handbook of the learning sciences,* 317-334. New York: Cambridge University Press.

Krashen, S. D. (1981). Bilingual education and second language acquisition theory. In Bilingual Bicultural Education, California State Department of Education (Ed.), *Schooling and language minority students: A theoretical framework* (pp. 51-79). Los Angeles: California State University, Evaluation, Dissemination and Assessment Center.

Krashen, S., & Bland, J. (2014). Compelling comprehensible input, academic language and school Libraries. *Children's Literature in English Language Education, 2*(2), 1-12.

Ladousse, G. P. (1987). *Role play.* Oxford: Oxford University Press.

Lee, H. (1999). *To kill a mockingbird (40th anniversary ed.).* New York: HarperCollins Publishers.

Long, M. H. (1983). Native speaker/non-native speaker conversation and the negotiation of comprehensible input. *Applied Linguistics, 4*(2), 126-141.

Lopez, M. M. (2008). *'Aqui en los estados unidos hablamos ingles....o, y espanol tambien': Students' emerging language ideologies and literacy practices in a dual language primary program.* (Doctoral Dissertation). San Antonio, TX: University of Texas at San Antonio. Retrieved from: http://www.academia.edu/761909/_Aqui_en_los_Estados_Unidos_hablamos_ingles...._o_y_espanol_tambien_Students_emerging_language_ideologies_and_literacy_practices_in_a_dual_language_primary

Moll, L. C., Amanti, C., Neff, D., & González, N. (1992). Funds of knowledge for teaching: Using a qualitative approach to connect homes and classrooms. *Theory into Practice, 31*(2), 132-141.

Montessori, M. (1936). *The secret of childhood.* B. B. Carter (Ed.). Calcutta: Orient Longmans.

Murphey, T. (1990). *Song and music in language learning: An analysis of pop song lyrics and the use of song and music in teaching English as a foreign language.* (Doctoral Dissertation). Bern, Switzerland: Peter Lang's European University Studies in Education, series X1.

Nessel, D. D., & Dixon, C. N. (2008). *Using the language experience approach with English language learners: Strategies for engaging students and developing literacy.* Thousand Oaks, CA: Corwin Press.

Nieto, S. (2015). *The light in their eyes: Creating multicultural learning communities.* New York: Teachers College Press.

Olsen, L. (2014). *Meeting the unique needs of long term English language learners: A guide for educators.* Washington, DC: National Education Association. Retrieved from: http://www.nea.org/assets/docs/15420_LongTermEngLangLearner_final_web_3-24-14.pdf

Ovando, C. J., Combs, M. C., & Collier, V. P. (2005). Bilingual and ESL classrooms: Teaching in multicultural contexts. New York: McGraw-Hill Education.

Park, L. S. (2016). *The day it rained cats.* New York: Scholastic Scope Magazine.

Peregoy, S. F., & Boyle, O. F. (2013). *Reading, Writing and Learning in ESL: A resource book for teaching k-12 English learners (6th ed.).* Boston, MA: Pearson Education.

Pérez, A. I. (2000). *Mi propio cuartito.* San Francisco, CA: Children's Book Press.

Salva, C., & Matis, A. (2017). *Boosting achievement: Reaching students with interrupted or minimal education.* Irving, TX: Seidlitz Education.

Seidlitz, J., Base, M., & Lara, M. (2016). *ELLs in Texas: What teachers need to know (2nd ed.).* Irving, TX: Seidlitz Education.

Seidlitz, J., & Perryman, B. (2011). 7 steps to a language-rich interactive classroom: Research-based strategies for engaging all students. Irving, TX: Seidlitz Education.

Shelley, P. B. (1962). Ozymandias. *Keats-Shelley Journal, 11,* 72-72.

Tomlinson, C. A. (2014). *The differentiated classroom: Responding to the needs of all learners (2nd ed.).* Alexandria, VA: ASCD.

Williams, L. (1969). *The little red hen.* Upper Saddle River, NJ: Prentice-Hall.

Williamson, V. J., Jilka, S. R., Fry, J., Finkel, S., Müllensiefen, D., & Stewart, L. (2012). How do "earworms" start? Classifying the everyday circumstances of involuntary musical imagery. *Psychology of Music, 40*(3), 259-284.

Wright, W. E. (2015). *Foundations for teaching English language learners: Research, theory, policy, and practice.* Philadelphia, PA: Caslon Incorporated.

Wright, W. E. (2016). Let them talk! *Educational Leadership, 73*(5), 24-29.

A second language learner herself, Dr. Lora Beth Escalante understands the joys and frustrations that accompany language acquisition. She has worked in the education field for over 16 years. Her current role is an Educational Consultant with Seidlitz Education. Her previous educational roles include: elementary ESL, bilingual and dual language teacher, university instructor, secondary instructional coach, and educational film producer. Her research includes student engagement through motivational strategies.

SEIDLITZ   PRODUCT ORDER FORM

Three ways to order

- **FAX** completed order form with payment information to **(949) 200-4384**
- **PHONE** order information to **(210) 315-7119**
- **ORDER ONLINE** at **www.seidlitzeducation.com**

Pricing, specifications, and availability subject to change without notice.

PRODUCT	PRICE	QTY	TOTAL$
NEW! ¡Toma la Palabra! SPANISH	$32.95		
NEW! Pathways to Greatness for ELL Newcomers: A Comprehensive Guide for Schools & Teachers	$32.95		
NEW! Teaching Social Studies to ELLs	$24.95		
NEW! Boosting Achievement: Reaching Students with Interrupted or Minimal Education	$26.95		
NEW! ELLs in Texas: What Teachers Need to Know 2ND EDITION	$34.95		
ELLs in Texas: What Administrators Need to Know 2ND EDITION	$29.95		
NEW! Talk Read Talk Write: A Practical Routine for Learning in All Content Areas K-12 2ND EDITION	$32.95		
Vocabulary Now! 44 Strategies All Teachers Can Use	$29.95		
Diverse Learner Flip Book	$26.95		
ELPS Flip Book	$19.95		
Academic Language Cards and Activity Booklet, ENGLISH	$19.95		
Academic Language Cards, SPANISH	$9.95		
RTI for ELLs Fold-Out	$16.95		
7 Steps to a Language-Rich Interactive Classroom	$29.95		
7 Pasos para crear un aula interactiva y rica en lenguaje SPANISH	$29.95		
38 Great Academic Language Builders	$24.95		
COLUMN 1 TOTAL $			

PRODUCT	PRICE	QTY	TOTAL$
NEW! Sheltered Instruction in Texas: A Guide for Teachers of ELLs	$26.95		
NEW! 7 Steps To a Language-Rich, Interactive **Foreign Language Classroom**	$32.95		
38 Great Academic Language Builders	$24.95		
Navigating the ELPS: Using the Standards to Improve Instruction for English Learners	$24.95		
Navigating the ELPS: Math (2nd Edition)	$29.95		
Navigating the ELPS: Science	$29.95		
Navigating the ELPS: Social Studies	$29.95		
Navigating the ELPS: Language Arts and Reading	$34.95		
'Instead Of I Don't Know' Poster, 24" x 36" ☐ Elementary ENGLISH ☐ Secondary ENGLISH	$9.95		
Instead Of I Don't Know Poster, 24" x 36" SPANISH (Elementary only)	$9.95		
Please Speak In Complete Sentences Poster 24" x 36" ☐ ENGLISH ☐ SPANISH	$9.95		
20 pack Instead Of I Don't Know Posters, 11" x 17" ☐ Elementary ENGLISH ☐ Secondary ENGLISH	$40.00		
20 pack Instead Of I Don't Know Posters, 11" x 17" SPANISH (Elementary only)	$40.00		
20 pack Please Speak In Complete Sentences Posters, 11" x 17" ☐ ENGLISH ☐ SPANISH	$40.00		
COLUMN 2 TOTAL $			

COLUMN 1+2	$
DISCOUNT	$
SHIPPING	$
TAX	$
TOTAL	**$**

SHIPPING 9% of order total, minimum $14.95
5-7 business days to ship. If needed sooner please call for rates.
TAX EXEMPT? please fax a copy of your certificate along with order.

NAME

SHIPPING ADDRESS   CITY   STATE, ZIP

PHONE NUMBER   EMAIL ADDRESS

TO ORDER BY FAX to **(949)200-4384** please complete credit card info **or** attach purchase order

☐ Visa   ☐ MasterCard   ☐ Discover   ☐ AMEX

CARD #   EXPIRES
                               mm/yyyy
SIGNATURE   CVV
                              3- or 4- digit code

☐ **Purchase Order attached**
please make P.O. out to **Seidlitz Education**

For information about Seidlitz Education products and professional development, please contact us at

(210) 315-7119 | kathy@johnseidlitz.com
56 Via Regalo, San Clemente, CA 92673
www.seidlitzeducation.com

Giving kids the gift of **academic language.™**

REV032918

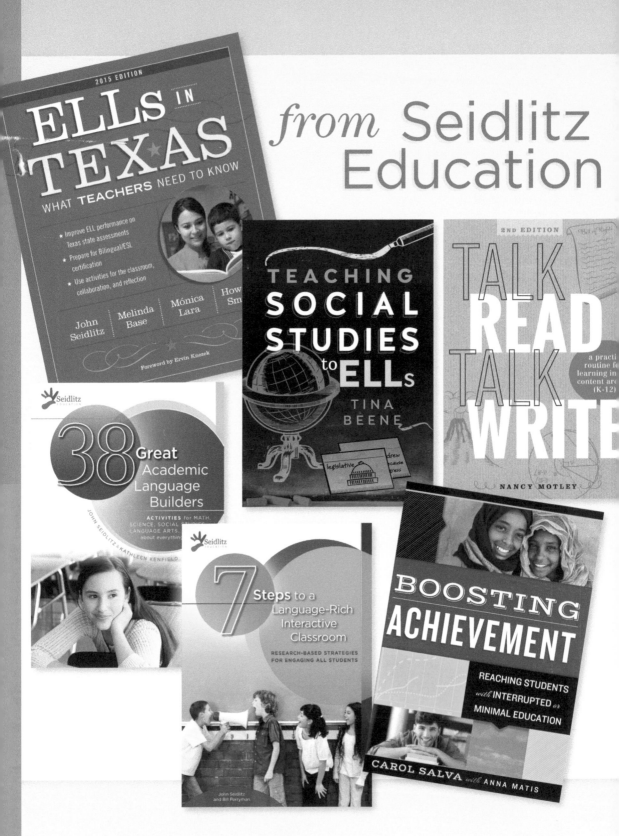